First Illustrated Dictionary

Schofield & Sims

Published by Schofield and Sims Limited, Dogley Mill, Fenay Bridge, Huddersfield HD8 0NQ, UK
Telephone 01484 607080

www.schofieldandsims.co.uk

Original edition first published in 1993
This revised and updated edition first published in 2009

British Library Cataloguing in Publication Data
A catalogue record for this book is available from the British Library.

Editorial project management by
Carolyn Richardson Publishing Services (cr@publiserve.co.uk)

Design by **Oxford Designers & Illustrators**

Printed in the UK by **Wyndeham Gait Ltd**, Grimsby, Lincolnshire

ISBN 978 0 7217 1132 4

How to use this book

The words in dark blue are called **headwords**. They are shown in the same order as the letters of the alphabet. This order is called alphabetical order.

The **guide word** in this corner tells you the first word on this page.

The big red letters show the start of a **new section**.

The **picture** helps you to understand the headword.

This word changes when it describes more than one thing. The **plural** is given to help you. The plural is in dark blue, but it does not stand out as much as the headword. Sometimes a plural is given because the picture shows more than one thing.

The **guide word** in this corner tells you the last word on this page. The guide words help you to find your way round the book.

The black words under a headword are called **definitions**. They tell you what the word means.

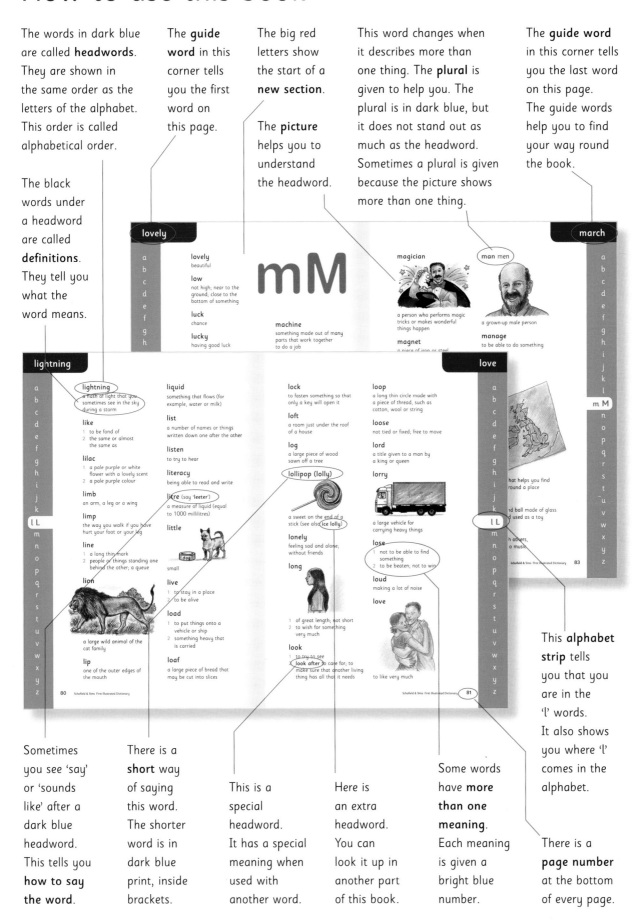

Sometimes you see 'say' or 'sounds like' after a dark blue headword. This tells you **how to say the word**.

There is a **short** way of saying this word. The shorter word is in dark blue print, inside brackets.

This is a special headword. It has a special meaning when used with another word.

Here is an extra headword. You can look it up in another part of this book.

Some words have **more than one meaning**. Each meaning is given a bright blue number.

This **alphabet strip** tells you that you are in the 'l' words. It also shows you where 'l' comes in the alphabet.

There is a **page number** at the bottom of every page.

aA

able

having the skill to do something

accident

something (bad) that happens by chance

acorn

the fruit of the oak tree

acrobat

someone who does leaping and balancing tricks

act

1 to do something
2 a part of a play
3 to perform on stage

actor

a man or woman who performs in a play, a film or on television

add

2+2

1 to find the total of two or more numbers (+)
2 to put together with something else

address

the building, street and town where you live

admire

to think well of someone or something

admit

1 to agree that something has happened or is true
2 to allow somebody or something to enter

adult

a grown-up person

adventure

an exciting happening

advise

to tell other people what you think they should do

aerial

a wire that sends out or picks up radio or television signals

aeroplane (plane)

a flying machine

affect

to make a change happen

afford

to be able to pay for

afraid

frightened; full of fear

afternoon

the time of the day between morning and evening

again

once more

against

1 on the opposite side to (in a game, for example)
2 next to and touching someone or something

age

how old you are

ago

in the past

agree

to think the same

aid

to help

aim

1 to point at
2 to try to do something

air

the gas that you breathe

airport

a place where planes land and take off

alarm

1 a warning bell or other sound
2 a sudden fright

alive

living; not dead

a **A**
b
c
d
e
f
g
h
i
j
k
l
m
n
o
p
q
r
s
t
u
v
w
x
y
z

allow
to let someone do something

almost
nearly; not quite

alone
by yourself

alphabet

letters in their special fixed order (for example, a, b, c)

already
1   by this time
2   before this

alter
to make something different; to change

altogether
counting everybody or everything

always
for ever; at all times

amazing
very surprising

ambulance

a van used to carry people who are ill or have been hurt

amount
a quantity; a sum of money

amuse
to make someone laugh or smile

anchor (say 'angker')

a heavy weight that is dropped into the sea when the crew wants a ship to stop moving

angel
someone who is believed to bring messages from God

angry
in a bad temper

animal
a living creature that can move

ankle

the joint between the leg and the foot

annoy

to make somebody upset or angry

answer

what you say or write when asked a question

ant

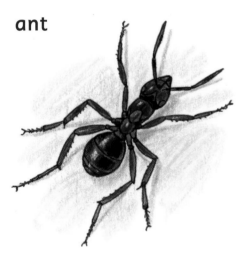

a tiny insect that lives in large groups

antelope

an animal like a deer, found in Africa

any

one of many; some

apple

a round hard fruit

apron

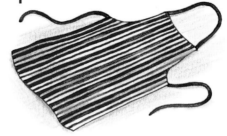

something you wear over your clothes to keep them clean

aquarium

a glass or plastic container in which fish are kept

arch

1   part of a building or bridge with a curved top and straight sides
2   to bend your body

area

1   a piece of land or sea
2   the size of a surface

argument

an angry talk; a fight with words

arm

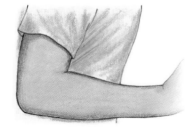

the part of the body between the shoulder and the hand

a A
b
c
d
e
f
g
h
i
j
k
l
m
n
o
p
q
r
s
t
u
v
w
x
y
z

armour

a covering of metal worn by
soldiers in battle in the old days

army

a large number of soldiers

arrange

1 to put things in order
2 to make plans to
   do something

arrest

to make someone a prisoner

arrive

to reach the place
you are going to

arrow

1 the straight, sharp piece of
   wood that is shot from a bow
2 a sign shaped like an
   arrow to show direction

art

the making of pictures
or sculptures

artist

a person who makes
pictures or sculptures

ash

1 the grey powder
   left after a fire
2 a kind of large tree

ashamed

feeling bad about something
you have done or not done

ask

1 to put a question to
2 **ask for** to say that
   you want something

asleep

sleeping

astronaut

a person who flies
in a spaceship

atlas

a book of maps

atmosphere

the air round the earth

attack

to hurt someone or
to start a fight

attract

1 to win the liking of
2 to make things come closer

audience

those who listen to or watch people performing (in a play, for example)

aunt (auntie, aunty)

a father's or mother's sister; the wife of an uncle

author

a person who writes books

autumn

the season between summer and winter

awake

not sleeping

away

not here; not present

awful

very bad

axe

a sharp piece of metal on a long handle, used for chopping wood

b B

baby

a very young child

back

1 the part furthest from the front
2 the part of the body between your neck and your bottom

bacon

salted or smoked meat from the back or sides of a pig

bad

not good

badge

a special sign you wear (to show your school or club, for example)

badger

an animal that has a black-and-white face and burrows in the ground

a
b B
c
d
e
f
g
h
i
j
k
l
m
n
o
p
q
r
s
t
u
v
w
x
y
z

bag

a soft container with a top that can be opened

bake

to cook in an oven

balance

1 to stay steady
2 a piece of equipment that weighs things

ball

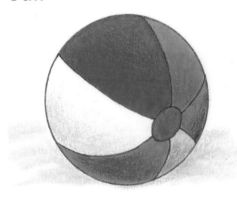

1 a round object, often used in games
2 a special event with dancing

ballet

a graceful dance that may tell a story

balloon

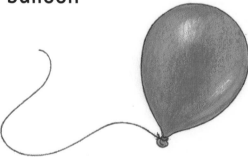

1 a toy of thin rubber that can be blown up
2 a round bag that rises when filled with hot air or gas

ban

not to allow something

banana

a long curved fruit with a yellow skin

band

1 a group of people who make music
2 a strip of material used to make something look pretty or to hold things together
3 a group of people

bandage

a strip of material used to wind round a cut or wound to protect it

bang

1 a sharp blow
2 a sudden loud noise

bank

1 the side of a river
2 a place where money is looked after
3 a pile of earth or sand with sloping sides

bar

1 a rod of metal or wood
2 a division in music
3 a counter where
   drinks are served

barbecue (BBQ)

a grill used to cook food outside

bare

1 having no clothes
   or covering on
2 empty

bark

1 the noise made by a dog
2 the hard covering round
   a tree or branch

barn

a building on a farm used to
store crops (for example, grain)

basin

a round and wide
container, usually used
for washing things in

basket

a bag or container made of
woven strips of straw or wood

basketball

a game in which two teams
try to throw a ball through
a high metal hoop

bat

1 the piece of wood used to
   strike a ball in some games
2 a small mouse-like animal
   that flies at night

bath

a water container that you can
lie or sit in to wash yourself

bathe

1 to swim or play in water
2 to wash

battery

a closed container that
stores electricity

battle

a fight between two large
groups of people

bay

a place where the
shore curves in

a
b B
c
d
e
f
g
h
i
j
k
l
m
n
o
p
q
r
s
t
u
v
w
x
y
z

a
b B
c
d
e
f
g
h
i
j
k
l
m
n
o
p
q
r
s
t
u
v
w
x
y
z

beach

land by the sea, covered
with sand or small stones

bead

a small piece of coloured
glass, wood or plastic that can
be threaded onto a string

beak

the hard, pointed
mouth of a bird

bean

a seed of the bean
plant, used for food

bear

a large hairy animal with
very strong teeth and claws

beard

hair growing on a man's chin

beat

1 to hit again and again
2 to keep time in music
3 to do better than someone
   else in a game

beautiful

very pretty; very pleasant
to see or hear

bed

1 a piece of furniture
   for sleeping on
2 a part of a garden where
   plants are grown

bee

an insect that makes honey
and can sting you

beech

a kind of tree with
smooth, grey bark

beetle

an insect with wings that
fold to make a hard cover
when it is not flying

beg

to ask someone for
money or things

begin

to start

behave

to act in a certain way, especially to act well towards others

behind

at the back of; on the other side of

believe

to feel sure that something is true; to trust in something

bell

1 a piece of metal, rounded like a cup, that rings when you swing or hit it
2 a device that you ring to say that you need something

belong

1 to be your own
2 to be a part of

below

lower down; under

belt

a narrow strip of material or leather, worn round the waist

bench

1 a long wooden seat
2 a work table

bend

1 a turn; a curve in a road
2 to make something curved

berry

a small fruit with juice inside

beside

at the side of; next to

better

1 finer than; nicer than
2 less ill than you were

between

1 in the middle of (two things, people or times, for example)
2 shared by two people

bicycle (bike)

a two-wheeled machine that you sit on to ride

a
b B
c
d
e
f
g
h
i
j
k
l
m
n
o
p
q
r
s
t
u
v
w
x
y
z

a
b B
c
d
e
f
g
h
i
j
k
l
m
n
o
p
q
r
s
t
u
v
w
x
y
z

big

large in size; the opposite of small

bill

1 a piece of paper that shows how much money you owe
2 the beak of a large bird

bin

a large container for putting rubbish in

bird

an animal with feathers and wings

birthday

the day of the year when a person was born

biscuit

a dry thin cake

bit

a small piece

bite

to cut something with the teeth

bitter

tasting sour; not sweet

black

the darkest colour; the opposite of white

blackbird

a kind of bird; the male has black feathers

blackboard

a dark board that you can write on with chalk

blade

the part of a tool that is used for cutting

blanket

a large warm covering, often made of wool

blaze

to burn with bright flames

blazer

a kind of jacket, which
may have a badge on it

bleed

to lose blood

blind

1 not able to see
2 a covering for a window

blink

to open and close
the eyes quickly

blister

a sore swelling on the skin
with liquid inside it

block

1 a thick piece of something
such as wood or stone
2 to be in the way of
3 one part of a large building
or group of buildings

blood (say 'bl**ud**')

the red liquid that moves
round your body

blossom

the flowers on plants and trees

blow

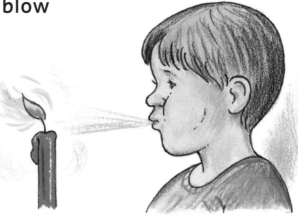

1 to shoot air out of the mouth
2 a hit made with the
hand or a weapon

blue

the colour of the sky
without clouds

bluebell bluebells

a wild flower; in spring
it has small blue flowers
shaped like bells

blunt

not able to cut; not sharp

blush

to go red because you are
ashamed, excited or shy

board

a flat piece of wood

a
b B
c
d
e
f
g
h
i
j
k
l
m
n
o
p
q
r
s
t
u
v
w
x
y
z

boast

to speak too proudly about yourself or about something that is yours

boat

a small ship

body

1 the whole of a person or animal
2 the main part of the body, not counting the head, arms and legs

boil

1 to cook in hot water
2 to heat water until it starts turning into steam
3 a painful swelling on the body

bolt

1 a sliding metal bar that keeps a door shut
2 a metal screw
3 to fasten a door
4 to do something suddenly and very fast

bomb

a weapon that is made to explode

bone

one of the hard parts of the body that make up the skeleton

bonfire

a large fire built in the open air

book

1 a number of pages joined together
2 to arrange for a seat to be kept for you (at the cinema, for example)

boot

1 a foot covering that comes above the ankle
2 a place at the back of a car where you can put bags

border

the edge of something

born

when something or somebody is first alive

borrow

to use something belonging to someone else and give it back later

bottle

a container for liquids, usually with a narrow neck

bottom

1 the lowest part of something
2 the part of your body that you sit on

bounce

to make something spring up and down

bow (sounds like 'low')

1 a knot with two loops on it
2 a weapon used to fire arrows
3 the special stick used when playing a violin

bow (sounds like 'now')

1 the front part of a boat
2 to bend forward from the waist in front of people you think are important

bowl

1 a deep round dish
2 in a ball game (cricket, for example) to throw the ball towards the person holding the bat

box

1 a container, usually with a lid; often made of wood, plastic, cardboard or metal
2 to fight with the fists

boy

a young male child

bracelet

something pretty that is worn round the wrist or arm

brag

to boast a lot

brain

the part of the head used for thinking

a
b B
c
d
e
f
g
h
i
j
k
l
m
n
o
p
q
r
s
t
u
v
w
x
y
z

a
b B
c
d
e
f
g
h
i
j
k
l
m
n
o
p
q
r
s
t
u
v
w
x
y
z

brake

the part of a vehicle that makes it go slower or stop

branch

the part of a tree on which the leaves grow

brave

not afraid; ready to face up to danger or pain

bread

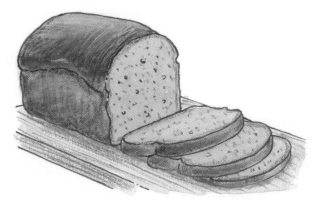

a baked food made from flour

break

1 to make something fall to pieces or damage something so it stops working
2 a short rest from what you are doing

breakfast

the first meal of the day

breath

air taken in and let out of your lungs

breathe

to take air in and let it out of your lungs

brick

1 a baked clay block used for building
2 a plastic or wooden block used as a toy

bride

a woman on her wedding day

bridegroom (groom)

a man on his wedding day

bridesmaid

a girl or young woman who helps the bride at a wedding

bridge

1 something built to let you cross over a river, road or railway
2 where the captain stands on a ship

bright

1 shining
2 clever

brim

1 the top edge of a container such as a basin
2 the part of a hat that sticks out at the edge

bring

to take with you

broad

very wide

brother

a boy or man who has the same parents as someone else

brown

the colour of earth and of chocolate

bruise

a mark on the skin where it has been hit

brush

1 something you use to tidy your hair
2 a kind of tool used for sweeping, scrubbing and painting
3 a fox's tail

bubble

a hollow ball of liquid filled with air or gas

bucket

a container with a handle, used for carrying liquids

bud

a leaf or flower before it opens

budgerigar (budgie)

a small brightly-coloured bird often kept as a pet

bug

1 a small insect
2 an illness
3 a mistake that makes a computer go wrong

buggy

a pushchair that folds up flat

a
b B
c
d
e
f
g
h
i
j
k
l
m
n
o
p
q
r
s
t
u
v
w
x
y
z

build

to put up; to make into something

building

something with walls and a roof

bulb

1 a root that is shaped like an onion
2 the part of an electric light that shines

bull

a male cow, elephant or whale

bulldozer

a large vehicle used for moving earth

bullet

a small piece of metal shot from a gun

bully

someone who hurts or frightens other people

bump

1 a sudden knock
2 a swelling on the body where it has been hit

bun

a small round bread roll or cake

bunch

several things tied together

bundle

many things tied or held together

bungalow

a house with no upstairs floors

bunk bed

two beds, one fixed above the other

burger

minced meat, grilled and served in a bun

burglar

a person who enters houses and shops to steal

burial (say 'berrial')

the burying of a dead body

burn

1 to be on fire or to set on fire
2 a place where your skin is sore because something hot has damaged it

burrow

a tunnel dug under the ground by an animal (a rabbit, for example)

burst

1 to blow into pieces
2 to break open

bury (say 'berry')

to put something in a hole in the ground and cover it over

bus

a large vehicle that carries lots of passengers

bush

a small tree

bushy

very thick

busy (say 'bizzy')

having no time to spare; doing a lot of things

butcher

a person who sells meat

butter

a fatty food made from cream; you can put it on bread

buttercup

a bright yellow wild flower

butterfly

an insect with four large wings, which are sometimes brightly coloured

button

a small round object that is used to do up clothing

buy (say 'by')

to get something by giving money

buzz

a low sound that is like the sound made by some insects (for example, bees)

a b c d e f g h i j k l m n o p q r s t u v w x y z

a
b
c C
d
e
f
g
h
i
j
k
l
m
n
o
p
q
r
s
t
u
v
w
x
y
z

cC

cabbage

a large vegetable with wide leaves that together make a ball shape

café (say 'caffay')

a place for eating simple meals or snacks

cage

a box or room made of wires or bars in which animals or birds are kept

cake

a sweet food made of fat, flour, eggs and sugar and baked in an oven

calculator

a small electronic machine used for solving number problems

calendar

a printed sheet or book listing the days and months of the year

calf

1 a young animal, usually a young cow or bull
2 the soft back part of the leg between the knee and ankle

call

1 to shout to
2 to visit
3 to give a name to

calm

quiet and still; peaceful

camel

a large animal with a hump, used for carrying people and goods in the desert

camera

a piece of equipment for taking photographs

camp

1 to live in a tent
2 a group of tents together

can

a small sealed container made of metal

canal

a long narrow ditch filled with water for boats to use

candle

a stick of wax with a string in the middle, which is burned to give light

canoe (say 'canoo')

a light boat moved by using a paddle

cap

1 a soft hat with a flat brim at the front only
2 a lid or cover

capacity

how much something holds

capital

1 the most important city or town
2 a large letter such as A

captain

1 the person who controls a plane or a ship
2 a person who is in charge of others in the army
3 the leader of a team or group

car

a vehicle that will carry about five people

caravan

a small house on wheels, which can be pulled by a vehicle

card

1 a piece of stiff paper
2 a piece of card with a message and often a picture
3 one of a set of cards used for playing games

cardboard

strong thick paper

cardigan

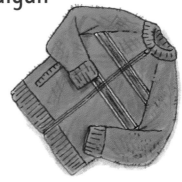

a knitted wool jacket

a b c **C** d e f g h i j k l m n o p q r s t u v w x y z

a
b
c C
d
e
f
g
h
i
j
k
l
m
n
o
p
q
r
s
t
u
v
w
x
y
z

care

1 to feel that someone or something is important to you
2 the act of looking after someone or something

careful

doing something with care; thinking about what you are doing and trying to do it well

caretaker

a person who looks after a building (a school, for example)

cargo

things carried on a ship or plane

carol

a Christmas song

carpet

a thick soft covering for a floor

carrot

a long orange root vegetable

carry

to take from one place to another

cart

a vehicle for carrying things, sometimes pulled by a horse

cartoon

1 a funny drawing in a magazine, book or newspaper
2 a film made out of drawings

case

1 a kind of box used to keep or carry things in
2 a suitcase

cash

money in notes or coins

castle

a stone building (usually old) with strong walls, built to keep out enemies

cat

a small furry animal often kept as a pet

catch

1 to take hold of
2 to get an illness

caterpillar

a creature that looks like a coloured worm with legs, and will turn into a moth or butterfly

cattle

a group of cows

cauliflower

a vegetable with a large white flower that you can eat

cautious (say 'corshus')

taking great care

cave

a hollow place in rocks or under the ground

CD

see **compact disk**

ceiling

the top part of a room; the roof of a room

cellar

a room under a building, used for storing things

cement

a stone powder that sets hard when mixed with water

centimetre

a measure of length; 100 centimetres are equal to one metre

centre

1 the middle of something
2 a place where people come together to do things

century

100 years

cereal

1 a kind of food made from grain and usually eaten for breakfast
2 a crop that is used for food (for example, wheat or rice)

certain

1 sure
2 to do with one special group of people or things and no others

chain

a number of rings joined together

chair

a piece of furniture for one person to sit on

chalk

1 a soft white rock that crumbles
2 a white or coloured stick used for writing on a blackboard

a
b
c C
d
e
f
g
h
i
j
k
l
m
n
o
p
q
r
s
t
u
v
w
x
y
z

champion

the winner of a competition

chance

1 an unexpected happening
2 a time when you can do something you want to do

change

1 to start being different
2 money you get back when you pay more than is needed

chapatti

a thin pancake made of bread (an Asian food)

chapter

a part of a story or book

charge

1 the amount you have to pay for something
2 **in charge of** in control of

chase

to run after

chat

to talk in a friendly way

chatter

to speak quickly, especially about things that do not matter much

cheap

low in price; not costing a lot

cheat

to act unfairly, break the rules or make others believe what is not true

check

1 to make sure that everything is correct
2 a pattern of squares

cheek

1 one of the sides of the face between the nose and the ears
2 rudeness

cheer

to shout loudly for joy

cheerful

full of fun; looking happy

cheese

a solid food made from milk

chef

the cook in a restaurant

chemist

someone who sells medicines

cherry

a small red or black fruit with a hard seed called a stone

chess

a board game played by two people on a squared board

chest

1 a large strong box
2 the upper front part of the body

chestnut

the hard brown fruit of the chestnut tree

chew

to bite food inside your mouth until it is small enough to swallow

chick

a young bird

chicken

a young hen kept for its eggs and meat

chief

1 the person in charge
2 the most important

child children

a young boy or girl

chill

1 coldness
2 a slight cold that makes you shiver

chilli chillies

a small hot-tasting seed pod, sometimes used in sauces

chimney

a tall pipe that takes smoke away from a fire

chimpanzee

a kind of monkey without a tail

a b c C d e f g h i j k l m n o p q r s t u v w x y z

a
b
c C
d
e
f
g
h
i
j
k
l
m
n
o
p
q
r
s
t
u
v
w
x
y
z

chin

the part of the face
below the bottom lip

chip

1 a long piece of fried potato
2 a tiny piece broken from
something larger

chocolate

a sweet food or drink
made from cocoa seeds

choir

a group of people
singing together

choke

1 not to be able to breathe
because of something
in your throat
2 to block up

choose

to pick out what you want
from two or more things

chop

1 to cut into pieces
2 a slice of meat with
a bone in it

Christmas

Christian festival in December

church

a building in which
Christians worship God

cinema

a place where films are shown

circle

a round flat shape

circus

a travelling show of acrobats,
clowns and sometimes animals

city

a large town

clap

1 to slap the hands
together quickly
2 the sound made by thunder

class

people who are taught together

claw

the sharp hard nail of
a bird or an animal

clay

sticky earth from which bricks and pots may be made

clean

not dirty or dusty

clear

1 easy to see, hear or understand
2 to put away; to tidy

clever

1 quick at learning and understanding things
2 skilful

cliff

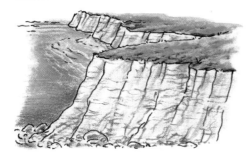

high steep land, often beside the sea

climb

to go up a steep place (a mountain or a hill, for example)

clinic

a place where doctors and nurses give help to people

clip

1 to cut with a pair of shears or scissors
2 something you use to join things together

clock

a machine that shows the time

close (sounds like 'dose')

near

close (sounds like 'doze')

to shut

cloth

1 material (for making clothes or curtains, for example)
2 a piece of cloth used for cleaning

clothes

things that you wear on your body (for example, trousers)

cloud

rainy mist or smoke that is floating in the sky

a
b
c C
d
e
f
g
h
i
j
k
l
m
n
o
p
q
r
s
t
u
v
w
x
y
z

clown

a person who acts foolishly
to make people laugh

club

1 a heavy stick
2 a group of people who meet
   together for a special reason
3 a stick used to play golf
4 one of the four kinds in a
   pack of playing cards

clue

something that helps you
to find the answer to a
puzzle or a question

clumsy

not very careful in the
way you move

coach

1 a passenger vehicle
   that is like a bus
2 a person who gives special
   training (to a football
   team, for example)

coal

a black rock dug out of
the ground and burned
to make heat

coat

1 a piece of clothing with
   sleeves, worn over
   other clothes
2 the hair of an animal

cobweb (web)

a net made by a spider
to trap insects

cocoa

1 a powder made from the
   seed of a cocoa tree
2 hot chocolate; a drink made
   from cocoa and milk or water

coconut coconuts

a hard and hairy fruit
that is white inside

cod

a large sea fish used as food

code

1 writing with a
   hidden meaning
2 a set of rules

coffee

a drink made from the roasted and crushed seeds of the coffee tree

coin

a piece of metal used as money

cold

1 not hot
2 an illness that makes your nose run

collar

1 a long piece of leather or metal put round the neck of an animal
2 the part of your clothes that fits round your neck

collect

to bring things together for a special reason

colour

one way of saying how things look (green or red, for example)

comb

a thin piece of metal or plastic with many teeth, used to keep hair tidy

comedy

a play or film that makes you laugh

comfort

1 to show kindness to someone in pain or trouble
2 a pleasant easy feeling

comfortable

giving or having comfort

comic

1 a magazine or paper for young people, with stories told in pictures
2 making you laugh; funny

common

ordinary; usual; found in many places

compact disk (CD)

a disk containing information, sounds or pictures

a b c C d e f g h i j k l m n o p q r s t u v w x y z

compass

an instrument that tells you where north is

competition

a way of finding out who is the best or luckiest at something

complain

to say that you are unhappy about something

composer

a person who makes up music

computer

a machine that stores information and can work things out quickly

concert

music played in front of an audience

cone

1 the fruit of the fir tree
2 a container for ice cream, wide at the top and pointed at the bottom

conjuror

a magician; someone who can do tricks

conscious

awake; knowing what is happening

contain

to have inside; to hold

container

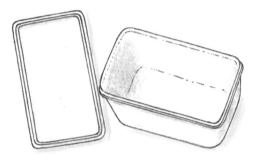

a box or jar that you can put things in

continue

to go on with; to go on; to last

control

to guide; to keep steady

cook

1 to make food ready to eat by heating it
2 a person who cooks

cool

not quite cold

copy

1 to do the same thing as somebody else
2 to make something the same as something else

cord

string that is thick and strong

core

the part in the centre of
something

cork

1 the light thick bark
   of the cork tree
2 a piece of this used to close
   the mouth of a bottle

corner

where two roads, lines
or walls meet

correct

quite right; true

cost

how much you must pay
to buy something

costume

clothes worn for a special reason

cot

a baby's bed with high sides

cottage

a small house, often in
the country

cotton

1 a kind of light cloth
   made from a plant grown
   in warm countries
2 thread used for sewing

couch

a soft seat made for more than
one person; a sofa; a settee

cough

to force air from the chest
and lungs with a noise

count

to number in the proper
order; to add up

counter

1 a table over which things
   are served in a shop
2 a small disc used in
   counting and in games

country

1 the part of a land that
   is away from towns
2 the whole of a land (for
   example, Germany or France)

courage

being brave

a
b
c C
d
e
f
g
h
i
j
k
l
m
n
o
p
q
r
s
t
u
v
w
x
y
z

a
b
c C
d
e
f
g
h
i
j
k
l
m
n
o
p
q
r
s
t
u
v
w
x
y
z

course

one part of a meal (for example, the dessert)

cousin

the child of an uncle or aunt

cover

to put something over something else

cow

1 a large female animal kept on farms for its milk and meat
2 the female of some other animals (for example, the elephant or the whale)

coward

a person who runs away from danger or difficulty

crab

a kind of shellfish with ten legs

crack

1 a thin break
2 a sharp noise like something hard breaking

crane

a tall machine for lifting heavy things

crash

1 to hit against and be smashed
2 a loud noise made by something breaking

crawl

1 to move on the hands and knees
2 to move slowly
3 a special way of swimming

crayon

a coloured pencil or a stick of coloured wax for drawing with

crazy

1 very foolish; without sense
2 likely to do strange or silly things

cream

1 liquid like milk but thicker
2 the colour of cream

creature

any living thing (for example, an animal of any kind, including birds, insects and fish)

crew

a team of people who do the work on a ship or a plane

cricket

a game played outside, using a ball and a bat

crime

breaking the law

crisp crisps

1 a very thin slice of potato cooked in oil and eaten as a snack
2 firm and dry

crocodile

a large and dangerous animal with a scaly skin; it is found in some hot countries, especially in rivers

crocus

a small spring flower that is yellow, purple or white

crook

a person who commits a crime; a criminal

crop

1 plants grown for food
2 the amount of these plants picked at one time
3 to cut something short (for example, hair)

cross

1 to move from one side to the other
2 anything shaped like a × or a +
3 angry

crow

a large black bird that has a loud rough cry

crowd

a large number of people all together in one place

crown

a large ring, often made of gold and jewels, that is worn on the head of a king or queen

a b c C d e f g h i j k l m n o p q r s t u v w x y z

a
b
c C
d
e
f
g
h
i
j
k
l
m
n
o
p
q
r
s
t
u
v
w
x
y
z

cruel

very unkind

crumb

a tiny piece of bread or cake

crush

to press together very tightly; to squash

crust

the hard outside part of anything, especially of bread

cry

1 to have tears coming from your eyes; to weep
2 to call out
3 a noise made by a person or an animal

cub

a young animal such as a fox, wolf or lion

cube

a solid square shape

cuckoo

a bird that lays its eggs in other birds' nests and makes a sound like its name

cuddle

to take into the arms and hug closely

cupboard

a set of shelves with doors at the front

cure

to make better somebody who has been ill

curious

1 strange; odd
2 wanting to know

curl curls

hair that falls into curves

curry

a hot-tasting Asian food made of meat and/or vegetables

curtain

a cloth that hangs in front of something (a window, for example)

curve

a smooth rounded shape
or a bend

cushion

a pillow that may be used
on a sofa or chair

custard

a sweet yellow sauce that
is eaten with puddings

customer

a person who pays money
for something (in a shop,
for example)

cut

to open or divide with
something sharp

cute

very pretty or sweet

cycle

1   a bicycle
2   to make a bicycle move

cylinder

a long round shape, like a can

dD

Daddy (Dad)

a name for your father

daffodil daffodils

a yellow spring flower
grown from a bulb

daisy

a small flower with a yellow
centre and white petals

dam

a wall built to hold back water

damage

to harm

damp

slightly wet

a
b
c
d D
e
f
g
h
i
j
k
l
m
n
o
p
q
r
s
t
u
v
w
x
y
z

a
b
c
d D
e
f
g
h
i
j
k
l
m
n
o
p
q
r
s
t
u
v
w
x
y
z

dance

to move the body to music

dandelion

a yellow wild flower

danger

harm; something that
can hurt you

dangerous

likely to hurt, harm or kill

dare

1 to be brave enough to do
   something dangerous
2 to ask someone to do
   something dangerous

dark

not light or bright

darling

a name for someone
you love very much

dart

1 to move very quickly
2 a small arrow thrown
   at a board in a game

date

1 the day, month and year
   when something takes place
2 a sweet brown fruit

daughter

a female child of a parent

dawdle

to do something so slowly
that time is wasted

dawn

the first light of the day;
early in the morning

day

1 a length of time of 24 hours
2 the time between
   sunrise and sunset

dead

no longer alive

deaf

not able to hear

dear

1 much loved by someone
2 costing a lot of money

decide

to make up your mind
about something

deck

the floor of a boat, a
plane or a bus

decorate

1 to paint the inside of a house
2 to make something prettier

deep

far down, often in water;
far inside

deer deer

a large wild animal that
can run fast

deliberate

done on purpose

delicious

having a very pleasant
taste or smell

den

the place where a wild
animal eats and sleeps

dentist

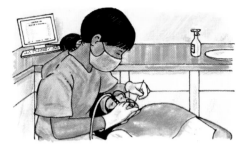

a person who looks after teeth

deny

to say firmly that something
is not true

describe

to say how something or
someone looks

desert (say 'desert')

a hot and dry place where
hardly anything grows

deserve

to have earned a reward
or punishment by what
you have done

desk

a kind of table used for
writing at

dessert (say 'dessert')

something sweet that you
eat at the end of a meal

a
b
c
d D
e
f
g
h
i
j
k
l
m
n
o
p
q
r
s
t
u
v
w
x
y
z

a b c **d D** e f g h i j k l m n o p q r s t u v w x y z

destroy

to break up completely

detail

a very small part or fact

detective

a person, usually a police officer, whose job it is to find out who carried out a crime

develop

to grow; to change gradually

device

an object that helps you to do something

dial

1 the face of an object such as a clock or watch, with numbers or letters on it
2 to press the numbers on a phone when you make a phone call

diamond

1 a very hard and sparkly jewel, often used in rings
2 a shape with four sloping sides that are the same length
3 one of the four kinds in a pack of playing cards

diary

a book in which you write what happens each day

dice

a small square block with spots on each side, used in many games

dictionary

a book like this one, with a list of words and their meanings arranged in the same order as the letters of the alphabet

die

to stop living

different

not like something else; not the same

difficult

not easy to do or to understand

dig

to turn soil over with a spade

dim

not bright; not easy to see

dinner

the main meal of the day

dinosaur

a large creature that lived millions of years ago

dip

1 to place into liquid for a short time
2 to slope downwards

direction

the way you are going or the way you are facing

dirt

mud; dust; something not clean

dirty

not clean

disabled

not able to use part of your body or mind

disagree

not to agree with

disappear

to go out of sight; to vanish

disappoint

to make somebody sorry because they have not got what they hoped for

disaster

a very bad event or accident

disc (sometimes spelt **disk**)

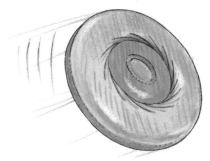

a round flat object (see also **compact disk**)

disco

a place where people dance to music

discover

to find out about something; to find for the first time

discuss

to talk about something with other people

disease

an illness

disguise

to change how you look by making your face look different and by changing your clothes

dish

a bowl or plate

a
b
c
d D
e
f
g
h
i
j
k
l
m
n
o
p
q
r
s
t
u
v
w
x
y
z

a
b
c
d D
e
f
g
h
i
j
k
l
m
n
o
p
q
r
s
t
u
v
w
x
y
z

dishwasher

a machine that washes dishes

disk

see **disc** and **compact disk**

distance

1 somewhere far away
2 the space between two points or places

ditch

a long narrow hole in the ground

dive

to jump head first, usually into water

divide

to share between; to separate; to put into different groups

division

separating something into parts (÷)

divorce

when a husband and wife decide to end their marriage

Diwali

the Hindu festival of lights

dizzy

unsteady; feeling as if you are spinning round

dock

a place where boats are loaded and unloaded

doctor

a person who looks after people's health

dodge

to move quickly from one side to the other; to keep away from

dog

a hairy animal that barks and is often kept as a pet

doll

a toy that looks like a small person

dolphin

a large animal that lives in the sea

domino

an oblong piece of plastic or wood with dots or pictures on it, used in the game dominoes

donkey

an animal like a small horse with very long ears

door

a flat piece of wood or other material that swings open to let you in (to a room, a wardrobe or a car, for example)

dot

a tiny round mark or point

double

twice the amount

doubt

not to be sure; to question

dough (say 'doe')

a soft mixture of flour and water

down

1 lower; below
2 soft hair or feathers

dozen

12; twelve

drag

to pull something over the ground

dragon

in stories, an animal with wings that has fire coming from its mouth

drain

to take liquid away from something

drama

1 a story that can be acted; a play
2 something that makes you feel excited

draught (say 'draft')

a cold stream of air entering a warmer room

a b c **d D** e f g h i j k l m n o p q r s t u v w x y z

a
b
c
d D
e
f
g
h
i
j
k
l
m
n
o
p
q
r
s
t
u
v
w
x
y
z

draughts (say 'drafts')

a game played with round pieces on a board with dark and light squares

draw

1 to make a picture in one colour only
2 a game that ends with equal scores

drawer

an open box with handles that fits into a piece of furniture

dreadful

very bad; terrible

dream

to see and hear things when you are asleep

dress

1 clothing like a skirt and top together, worn by women and girls
2 to put on your clothes

dressing gown

a soft coat worn over night clothes

drink

to swallow liquid

drip

to fall in drops

drive

to make something move (for example, a vehicle or an animal)

driver

someone who drives

drop

1 to fall from a high place
2 one tiny spot of liquid

drown

to die in water because you cannot breathe

drum

a musical instrument that is played by beating it with sticks

dry

not wet or damp

duck

1 a common water bird
2 to bend down quickly
   so as not to be hit

dull

1 not bright or shiny
2 not interesting

dumb (say 'dum')

unable to speak

dust

a fine dry powder that
is carried on the air

duties

the things people have
to do (as part of their
work, for example)

duvet (say '**doovay**')

a bed cover filled with soft
feathers or other material

DVD

a small disk containing
video or a movie

dwarf

a plant or animal that is
much smaller than most

eE

each

every one by itself

eagle

a large wild bird that kills
small animals for food

ear

the part of the head with
which you hear

early

1 before the time fixed
2 near the beginning

earn

1 to get money by working
2 to deserve

earring

jewellery worn on the ear

a
b
c
d
e E
f
g
h
i
j
k
l
m
n
o
p
q
r
s
t
u
v
w
x
y
z

a
b
c
d
e E
f
g
h
i
j
k
l
m
n
o
p
q
r
s
t
u
v
w
x
y
z

earth

1 the world in which you live
2 the soil in which things grow

earthquake

when part of the earth's
surface shakes

east

the direction from
which the sun rises

Easter

Christian festival in spring

easy

simple to do; not difficult
to understand

eat

to bite, chew and swallow food

echo

the sound that bounces back
to you in an empty place

edge

the rim; the border

eel

a kind of fish that looks
like a snake

effort

the use of all your strength or
skill in trying to do something

egg

the rounded object from which
some creatures are hatched
(for example, fish and birds)

Eid (say 'Eed')

Muslim festival at the
end of Ramadan

elastic

a material that will stretch and
then go back to its own length

elbow

the joint in the middle of
the arm

electricity

a form of energy that goes
through wires and is used
for heating, lighting or
driving things

electronic

needing electricity and a
computer chip to work

elephant

a very large animal with a
trunk and two tusks

e-mail

a message sent by computer

embarrass

to make someone feel
shy or ashamed

emergency

something very bad that needs
to be dealt with immediately

empty

with nothing at all inside

encourage

to act or speak in a way that
helps someone to do something

end

1 to finish
2 the last part of something

enemy

someone you fight against

energy

strength to do things

engine

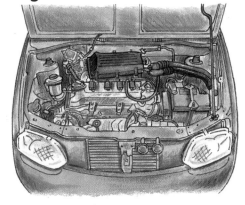

a machine that uses energy
(from electricity, petrol,
oil or steam, for example)
to make things move

enjoy

to like doing something
very much

enormous

very large

enough

as many or as much as needed

enter

to go into or to come into

entrance

the place where you enter;
the way in

entry

1 going or coming in
2 an entrance

a
b
c
d
e E
f
g
h
i
j
k
l
m
n
o
p
q
r
s
t
u
v
w
x
y
z

a
b
c
d
e E
f
g
h
i
j
k
l
m
n
o
p
q
r
s
t
u
v
w
x
y
z

envelope

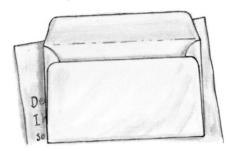

the paper cover in which a letter is placed

equal

1 exactly the same as (=)
2 just as good as

equipment

things that you need in order to do something

eraser

a small piece of rubber used for getting rid of marks on paper (also called a **rubber**)

escalator

moving stairs often found in shopping centres and airports

escape

to get away; to find a way out

especially

very; more than usual

even

1 flat and smooth
2 describes a number that can be divided by 2 (for example, 4, 6 and 8); not odd

evening

the time between afternoon and night

event

something that happens

every

each one of many

exaggerate

to say more than is really true

examine

to look at something carefully

excellent

very good

excited

very happy (when you are looking forward to something, for example)

excuse (sounds like 'l**oose**')

a reason for not doing what you should have done

excuse (sounds like 'n**ews**')

to forgive

exercise

moving your body in a way that keeps you fit (for example, walking or running)

exit

the way out of a place

expect

to think that something will happen

experiment

a test done on something to find out more about it

expert

a person who is very good at something or knows a lot about something

explain

to say clearly how something happened or what something is about so that people understand

explode

to blow up or burst with a loud noise

explore

to travel around; to search or examine a place carefully to find out more about it

export

to send goods out of a country

extra

1 in addition to
2 more than is needed or usual

eye eyes

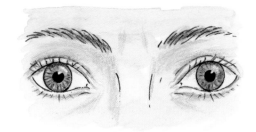

1 the part of the head with which you see
2 the hole in a needle

eyebrow

the line of hair that grows on your forehead above each eye

a
b
c
d
e E
f
g
h
i
j
k
l
m
n
o
p
q
r
s
t
u
v
w
x
y
z

a
b
c
d
e
f F
g
h
i
j
k
l
m
n
o
p
q
r
s
t
u
v
w
x
y
z

face

1 the front part of the head
2 the front of an object
3 one side of a shape
4 to turn towards something

fact

something that is true

factory

a place where things are
made by machines

fade

to lose colour; to get dimmer

fail

1 not to do something that
  you are expected to do
2 not to pass a test

faint

1 not clear; not easy to see
2 to lose your senses and
  to stop being conscious
  for a short time

fair

1 a market or a show that
  is held outside
2 light in colour; not dark
3 treating every
  person the same
4 neither good nor bad

fairground

an open area where fairs
are held

fairy

an imaginary person, often
tiny, who can use magic
to do special things

faith

feeling sure about something;
trusting somebody

faithful

true; to be trusted

fall

to drop; to come down;
to move lower down

false

not true; not real

family

a group of people who are related (for example, a father, a mother and their child or children)

famine

being without food for a very long time

famous

well known because of what you have done

fan

1 an instrument that makes air move and keeps you cool
2 a person who is very interested in something or someone (for example, a football team)

far

not near; a long way away

fare

money paid for a journey

farm

land used for growing crops and keeping animals

farmer

a person who owns or looks after a farm

fast

very quick; speedy

fasten

to tie or join things together

fat

1 very big all round; not thin
2 the grease from animals and plants that is used for cooking
3 the greasy part of meat

father (daddy, dad)

a male parent

a b c d e f F g h i j k l m n o p q r s t u v w x y z

fault

1 a mistake in the way something was made

2 something you do wrong that makes a bad thing happen

favour

something good you do for someone

favourite

the one that you like better than any of the others

fear

to be afraid of; to be frightened that something bad might happen

feast

a special meal for lots of people together

feather

one of the flat and very light pieces that cover a bird's body and wings

feed

to give food to

feel

1 to touch something to find out what it is like

2 to have a feeling (for example, sadness or happiness)

female

a person or an animal that can be a mother; a girl or a woman

fence

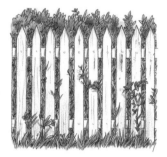

something built of wood or metal to separate one area from another

ferry

a boat that carries people and cars across water

festival

a special day on which lots of people enjoy themselves together

fetch

to go and get; to bring back what you were sent for

fever

an illness that makes the body hot

few

not many

fiction

a story about people or events that are not real

field

a piece of land with a hedge, fence or wall around it, where animals are kept or crops are grown

fierce

wild; cruel; angry

fight

a struggle or battle between two or more people

fill

to make full

film

1 a very thin covering
2 a story shown in a cinema or on television; a movie

fin

one of the thin flat parts of a fish that stick out from its body and help it to swim

final

1 the end; the last
2 the last match in a competition, which decides the winner

find

to come across something, usually something that you have been looking for

fine

1 when the weather is pleasant
2 very good; excellent
3 a sum of money paid as punishment for breaking the law

finger

one of the four longest parts of the hand

finish

to complete; to end

fire

1 the flames and heat that you see when something is burning
2 to shoot a gun

fire-fighter

a person whose job it is to prevent or put out fires and rescue people from them

a b c d e f F g h i j k l m n o p q r s t u v w x y z

a b c d e **f F** g h i j k l m n o p q r s t u v w x y z

firework

a container with powder that makes pretty coloured flames and sparks when lit

firm

fixed; not likely to move or change

first

1   coming before everyone or everything else
2   at the start

first aid

helping someone who has been hurt or is ill, before a doctor comes

fish

1   an animal that lives and breathes in water
2   to try to catch fish to eat or as a sport

fist

the hand and fingers closed tightly together

fit

1   in good health; well and strong
2   suitable
3   to be the right size for

fix

1   to put in place so that it will not move
2   to put right

fizzy

with a lot of bubbles

flag

a piece of cloth with a special pattern and colours that is the special sign of something (a country or a club, for example)

flame

the part of a fire that is bright and blazing

flare

to blaze up suddenly

flash

a bright light that comes and goes quickly

flask

a container for keeping things hot

flat

1 level; smooth; not sloping or bumpy
2 a set of rooms all on one floor, where people live
3 a sound that is just below the correct note in music

flavour

the taste of something

fleet

a number of ships together

float

to stay on the surface of water without sinking or to be held up gently by the air

flock

a number of animals of the same sort together, especially sheep or birds

flood

when water from rivers and lakes flows onto roads and fields that are usually dry

floor

1 the part of a room that you walk on
2 one level in a building

florist

a person who sells flowers

flour

wheat that has been crushed into a powder which is used for baking

flow

to move smoothly, like running water

flower

the part of a plant that has coloured petals and produces seeds or fruit

flu

an illness like a very bad cold that makes you shiver and hurt all over

fly

1 to move through the air, especially on wings or in a plane
2 a kind of small insect with wings

a b c d e f F g h i j k l m n o p q r s t u v w x y z

a
b
c
d
e
f F
g
h
i
j
k
l
m
n
o
p
q
r
s
t
u
v
w
x
y
z

foal

a young horse

foam

bubbles on the top of a liquid

fog

air that is thick with a mist made of very small water drops

fold

to bend something so that one part covers another

follow

to go after; to come after

fond

liking someone or something very much

food

what people, animals and plants take in to keep them alive

fool

1 to trick somebody
2 a person who behaves in a silly way

foolish

slightly stupid; silly

foot feet

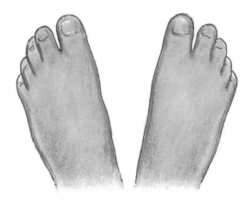

1 the part of the leg that you stand on
2 a measure of length (the same as about 30 centimetres)

football

1 a game played by two teams kicking a ball
2 a special ball for playing football

force

1 to make somebody do something; to make something happen
2 strength

forecast

to say what is likely to happen

forehead

the part of the head between your hair and your eyes

foreign (say 'for**un**')

belonging to another country

forest

a large area that is full of trees

forget

1 not to remember
2 to leave something behind

forgive

to stop being angry with someone even though they have done something wrong

fork

1 a small tool with long thin points for eating with
2 a large tool with a long handle and long thin points, used in the garden
3 where a road divides into two

fort

a strong building built to protect people from attack

fortnight

two weeks

fortunate

lucky

forward

towards the front

fox

a wild animal like a dog with a long thick tail

free

1 able to do as you wish
2 given away for nothing

freeze

to make or become very hard and cold; to turn to ice

freezer

a fridge that keeps things so cold that they stay frozen

fresh

1 new; newly picked or collected; just made
2 not tired

fridge

short for **refrigerator**

friend

somebody you like and can trust and enjoy doing things with

a
b
c
d
e
f F
g
h
i
j
k
l
m
n
o
p
q
r
s
t
u
v
w
x
y
z

a
b
c
d
e
f F
g
h
i
j
k
l
m
n
o
p
q
r
s
t
u
v
w
x
y
z

fright

sudden fear

fringe

short hair brushed forward
over the forehead

frog

a small jumping animal that can
live on land and in water

front (say 'fr**u**nt')

the part facing forward

frost

white powdery ice seen
in very cold weather

frown

to move your eyebrows down
and together to show that
you are angry or puzzled

frozen

very cold; made into ice

fruit

in some plants this is the place
where the seeds are found;
many fruits are good to eat
(for example, oranges)

fry

to cook in boiling fat or
oil in a pan

full

not able to hold any more

fun

enjoyable

funny

1   making you laugh
2   strange; odd

fur

the soft hairy covering
of some animals

furniture

chairs, tables, beds and
other such objects used
around your home

furry

having a soft hairy covering

future

the time yet to come

gG

gadget
a small object that does something useful

gallop
to move very fast on four legs, like a horse

game

1 something that you play; a sport
2 wild animals or birds that are hunted for food

gang
a group of people doing something together

gap
an opening between two places or things

garage
1 a place where cars are kept
2 a place where cars are repaired

garden

land where flowers, fruit or vegetables are grown

gas
1 something like air, which is neither liquid nor solid
2 a kind of gas that burns, used for heating and cooking

gate

a kind of door in a wall or a fence

gentle
soft; not rough; quiet and kind

gerbil

a small animal like a mouse, often kept as a pet

a b c d e f g G h i j k l m n o p q r s t u v w x y z

germ

a tiny living thing that can make you ill

ghost (sounds like 'toast')

a person that some people see or can feel even though that person is dead

giant

1 a huge person (for example, in a fairy story)
2 anything that is much larger than usual

gift

a present

giraffe

an African wild animal with a very long neck and long legs

girl

a female child or young woman

give

to hand over to someone else

glad

happy; pleased

glass

1 a hard material that you can usually see through
2 a cup that is without a handle and is made of glass

glasses

1 two pieces of glass or plastic, worn over your eyes to help you to see better
2 the plural of glass

glove

a covering for the hand with a separate place for each finger

glue

something used to stick things together

go

to move away; to leave

goal

1 a place you aim at in games (in football, for example)
2 the score made when the ball goes into the goal
3 something you hope to do in the future

goat

a farm animal with small horns

God

the person who is more important than all others; the person that people pray to

gold

a yellow metal that is very valuable

golden

1 looking like gold
2 made of gold

goldfish

a small orange fish, often kept as a pet

good

1 right; true
2 kind
3 well behaved

goodbye

something you say to people when you leave them

goose geese

a bird like a large duck

gorilla

a type of huge monkey that lives in the jungle

grab

to snatch; to grasp quickly

gradual

little by little

grain

the small hard seed of a cereal plant, used for food

gram

a small unit of mass

grammar

the rules to do with the words that people say or write

grand

very large and fine

a b c d e f **g G** h i j k l m n o p q r s t u v w x y z

a
b
c
d
e
f
g G
h
i
j
k
l
m
n
o
p
q
r
s
t
u
v
w
x
y
z

grandfather (grandpa, granddad)

the father of your
father or mother

grandmother (grandma, granny)

the mother of your
father or mother

grapes

small fruits with green or
purple skin and lots of juice;
grapes grow in a bunch

grass

the common green plant
that covers the ground
in fields and gardens

grave

1 a place in the ground
   where a person is buried
2 serious

gravy

a brown liquid eaten with meat

grease

1 animal fat
2 thick oil used to make
   machines run smoothly

great

1 big
2 important
3 very good

greedy

always wanting more;
never having enough

green

the colour of grass

grey

a colour that is in between
black and white

grill

1 to cook food by putting it very close to the heat (on a barbecue, for example)
2 the part of a cooker where you can grill food

grin

a wide smile

grip

to grasp tightly

ground

1 the surface of the earth; land
2 a place outside for playing certain games

group

a number of people, animals or things together

grow

1 to get bigger
2 to look after plants so that they get bigger

guard

1 to keep safe
2 a person whose job it is to protect something or someone
3 a person in charge of a train on its journey

guess

to say what you think might be correct without really knowing

guide

a person who shows you a place or shows you the way

guinea pig

a small furry animal with no tail that is usually kept as a pet

guitar

a musical instrument with six strings, played by pulling the strings and letting them go quickly

gun

a weapon from which bullets are fired

a
b
c
d
e
f
g
h H
i
j
k
l
m
n
o
p
q
r
s
·t
u
v
w
x
y
z

hH

hamster

a small animal like a large mouse, often kept as a pet

hail

frozen rain

hair

a thread-like covering that grows on the head and body

hairdresser

a person who cuts and arranges hair

half

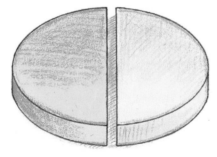

one of two equal parts of a thing

hall

1   a very large room where people meet
2   the room inside the front door of your home

hammer

a tool with a metal head used to hit nails (into wood, for example)

hand

1   the part of the arm below the wrist
2   a pointer on a clock

handkerchief (hanky)

a small piece of cloth for wiping your nose on

handle

1   to touch with the hand
2   the part of something that you hold in your hand

handlebars

the part of a bicycle that you use to steer it

handy

useful

happen

to take place

happy

feeling very pleased; glad

harbour

a place of shelter for boats

hard

1 difficult to do
2 tough; firm; not soft

hare

an animal like a large rabbit, with very long ears

harm

damage (to the body, for example)

harvest

1 a crop of food to be picked and brought in
2 the time when this is done

hat

a covering worn on the head

hatch

to be born from an egg

hate

to dislike very much

hawk

a large bird that hunts small birds or animals for food

hay

dried grass used as animal food

head

1 the part of the body above the neck
2 the person in charge
3 the front part or top of something

headphones

things you put over your ears to listen to music or speech without other people hearing

a
b
c
d
e
f
g
h H
i
j
k
l
m
n
o
p
q
r
s
t
u
v
w
x
y
z

a
b
c
d
e
f
g
h H
i
j
k
l
m
n
o
p
q
r
s
t
u
v
w
x
y
z

headteacher

the teacher in charge of a school

heal

to get well again after
being hurt

health

1 how you are, in body
   or mind
2 being well; being free
   from illness; fitness

hear

to catch the sound of;
to listen to

hearing aid

a device worn behind the
ear to help a person who
cannot hear very well

heart

1 the part of the body that
   sends the blood round
   the body
2 a shape with two rounded
   parts at the top and a
   sharp point at the bottom
3 one of the four kinds in a
   pack of playing cards

heat

1 warmth; being hot
2 one of the races leading
   to a final

heavy

having great weight

hedge

small bushes or trees grown in a
line to separate fields or gardens

hedgehog

a small animal with sharp pins
on its back that rolls itself
into a ball when in danger

heel

the back part of the foot

height

the distance from top to
bottom; how tall you are

helicopter

a plane that flies using large pieces of metal which go round and round very fast on its roof

helmet

a hard hat worn to protect the head from damage

help

to do something for another person

helpless

not able to do things yourself

hen

1 a kind of bird kept on a farm; its eggs and meat are used for food
2 a female bird

herbs

plants grown for use in cooking, to flavour food

herd

a large number of the same kind of animals living together

hide

1 to keep something in a secret place
2 to go where you cannot be found

high

tall; well above the ground

hijab

scarf worn over the head by Muslim women

hill

a high piece of land, often with steep sides

hippopotamus (hippo)

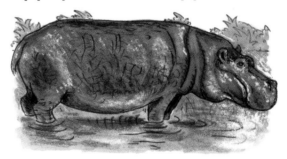

a large African wild animal that likes to wade in mud

history

what happened in the past

hit

to strike or knock something or someone

hive

the place where bees live

hobby

something you like doing in your spare time

a b c d e f g h H i j k l m n o p q r s t u v w x y z

a
b
c
d
e
f
g
h H
i
j
k
l
m
n
o
p
q
r
s
t
u
v
w
x
y
z

hold

1 to keep in your hand
2 to have inside; to contain

hole

an opening; a gap

holiday

a time when you are
free to go away

hollow

empty inside

holly

a green tree or bush with
prickly leaves and red berries

home

the place where you live

honest

to be trusted; truthful

honey

a sweet food made by bees

hoop

a ring of wood, plastic or metal

hoot

1 the sound made by a
car horn
2 the sound made by an owl

hop

to jump up and down
on one foot

hope

to wish or believe that
something you want will happen

horn

1 a sharp bone that grows out
of the head of some animals
2 a musical instrument
that you blow through

horrible

very unpleasant

horse

a large animal often
used to ride on

hospital

a place where sick people
are cared for

hot

very warm

hot dog

a long sausage in a bread roll

hotel

a building where you can pay to stay the night

hour

a length of time of 60 minutes; there are 24 hours in one day

house

a building in which people live

hovercraft

a vehicle that travels over water on a big cushion filled with air

howl

a long loud cry

huff

a bad mood

hug

to hold tightly in the arms

huge

very large

human

1 a person
2 to do with people

hunger

a great need, usually for food

hunt

to look very carefully for something

hurry

to move very quickly; to rush

hurt

1 to make someone feel pain
2 to feel pain

husband

a married man

hut

a small building or shed, usually made of wood

a b c d e f g h H i j k l m n o p q r s t u v w x y z

a
b
c
d
e
f
g
h
i I
j
k
l
m
n
o
p
q
r
s
t
u
v
w
x
y
z

iI

ice

frozen water

iceberg

a very large piece of ice floating in the sea

ice cream

a frozen food that is creamy, soft and sweet

ice lolly (lolly)

flavoured ice or ice cream on a stick

icicle

a pointed piece of ice that hangs down from something

icing

a sweet mixture sometimes spread over cakes and buns

idea

a thought; something in the mind

igloo

a house made of snow blocks

ignore

to deliberately take no notice of someone or something

ill

not well; sick

illness

what it is that is wrong with you when you are ill; a disease

imaginary

not real; made up

immediately

at once

important

mattering very much

impossible

not able to be done

in

when you are inside somewhere; the opposite of out

inch

a small measure of length (about two and a half centimetres); there are 12 inches in a foot

increase

to make larger or greater

infant

a baby; a young child

information

facts that you can learn about someone or something

insect

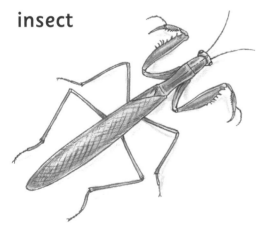

a very small creature with six legs

inside

the part that is in something else

instructions

words that tell you what to do or how to do it

instrument instruments

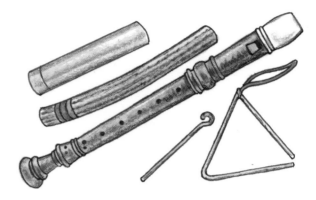

1   something on which music is played
2   a tool

interesting

worth knowing about

internet (net)

the place where you can find information using a computer (also called the **web**)

interval

a space between things

invent

to think of and make something for the first time

inventor

someone who invents things

invisible

not able to be seen

invitation

when someone asks you to do something (to go to a party, for example)

invite

to ask somebody to come to your house or to go out with you

iron

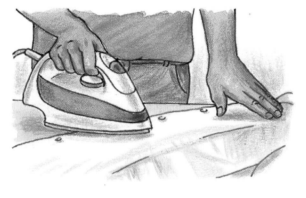

1 a tool for making clothes smooth
2 a hard strong metal

island

a piece of land with water all round it

itch

a tickling of the skin that makes you want to scratch

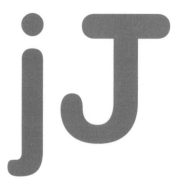

jacket

a short coat

jam

1 a food made from boiled fruit and sugar
2 when something is pressed together so that it cannot move any more (the traffic in a traffic jam, for example)

jar

a container with a wide opening at the top

jaw

the bone to which teeth are fixed; the lower part of the face

jealous

annoyed because you wish you had what others have

jeans

trousers made from strong cotton, often blue

jelly

a cold clear pudding

jet

1 a thin stream of water or air
2 a plane that can fly very fast because it has a special kind of engine

jewel

a valuable stone

jewellery

something special that you wear to make yourself look good (for example, a necklace, bracelet or ring)

jigsaw puzzle (jigsaw)

a kind of puzzle made of little pieces that you put together to make a picture

job

1 a piece of work
2 the work someone does to earn money

jog

to run for exercise

join

1 to fasten together
2 to start being a member of a group

joke

a funny story, usually quite short

journey

a trip from place to place

joy

happiness; gladness

joystick

a control stick for a plane or for computer or video games

a b c d e f g h i **j J** k l m n o p q r s t u v w x y z

a
b
c
d
e
f
g
h
i
j
k K
l
m
n
o
p
q
r
s
t
u
v
w
x
y
z

jug

a container for pouring liquids

juggler

a person who can keep several objects in the air at the same time without dropping them

juice

the liquid that comes from fruit and vegetables

jump

to spring up

jumper

a knitted garment worn on the top part of the body

jungle

a thick forest in a very hot country

kK

kangaroo

an Australian animal that jumps using its back legs

keen

liking something very much; wanting to do something, and wanting to do it well

kennel

a small house for a dog

kerb

the edge of the pavement

ketchup

a tomato sauce that is often eaten with burgers or chips

kettle

a container used to boil water

key

1 a tool to open or close a lock
2 a part that you press down on a musical instrument or a computer keyboard

keyboard

1 a flat plastic tray made up of buttons with letters and numbers on them; you press the buttons to type something on a computer
2 an electric piano

kick

to hit with the foot

kill

to make something or someone die

kilogram

a measure of mass equal to 1000 grams

kilometre

a measure of length equal to 1000 metres

kind

1 a type; a sort
2 good; helpful; gentle

king

a male head of a country

kiosk

a small hut from which something is sold (for example, tickets or newspapers)

kiss

to touch with the lips

kitchen

a room used for cooking

kite

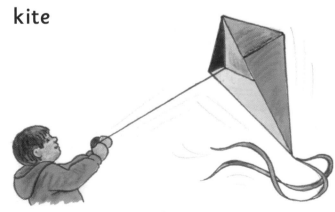

a toy that you fly outside at the end of a long string

kitten

a young cat

a b c d e f g h i j k K l m n o p q r s t u v w x y z

a b c d e f g h i j k **l L** m n o p q r s t u v w x y z

knee (say '**nee**')

the joint in the middle of the leg

knickers (say '**nickers**')

pants that girls and women wear

knife (say '**nife**')

a tool used for cutting

knit (say '**nit**')

to join loops of wool using long needles

knob (say '**nob**')

a round handle used on doors and taps

knock (say '**nock**')

1 to make a tapping noise
2 to strike hard

knot (say '**not**')

a fastening made by twisting and tying string or rope

know (say '**no**')

1 to have something in your mind
2 to have met someone before

label

paper or a card on which information can be written

ladder

a set of steps for getting up to high places

lady

a woman

ladybird

a small beetle, often red with black spots

lake

a large area of water with land all round it

lamb

a young sheep

lame

not able to walk easily

lamp
something made for giving light

land
the part of the earth not covered by the sea

lane
a narrow road

lantern

an old-fashioned lamp with a handle for carrying it

laptop
a computer that you can carry around with you

large
big; huge

lasagne (say 'lassanya')
an Italian meal made with pasta, meat and tomato sauce

last

1 coming after all the others
2 to go on for a length of time

late
coming after the right time

laugh

the sound you make when you are amused or happy

law
a rule that everyone must obey

lawn

an area of short grass in a garden

lay
1 to put down carefully
2 to put out knives and forks, ready for a meal
3 to make eggs

lazy
not fond of working; liking to do nothing

leader
the person in charge of a group

a b c d e f g h i j k l **L** m n o p q r s t u v w x y z

leaf

one of the flat green parts
of a plant

leak

liquid or gas that has escaped
through a hole or gap

leap

to jump; to spring

learn

to get to know; to get
better at doing something

leather

skin taken from an animal
and specially got ready
for making into things

leave

1 to go away from
2 to let something stay
    where it is

left

the opposite of right

leg

1 one of the limbs with
    which you walk
2 one of the supports at the
    corner of a chair or table

lemon

a yellow fruit with a sharp taste

lemonade

a sweet drink, usually fizzy

lend

to allow somebody to use
something that is yours

length

how long something is; the
distance from one end
to the other

lesson

something to be learned

let

to allow

letter

1 a written message sent
    to somebody by post
2 one of the signs you use for
    writing (for example, a, b, c)

lettuce

a vegetable with large green
leaves, used in salads

level

1 the same height from one end to the other; flat
2 equal

liar

a person who tells lies

library

a room or building where books are kept

lick

to wet something with your tongue; to move your tongue over something

lid

a cover that can be opened or taken off

lie

1 to stretch out flat (on a bed or on the floor, for example)
2 to say things that are not true
3 something that is not true

life

the time when you are alive

lifeboat

a special boat used to rescue people who are in danger at sea

lift

1 to raise
2 a machine that carries people or things up or down between the floors in a building
3 a ride in someone's vehicle

light

1 brightness that comes from the sun and from lamps and candles
2 pale in colour; not dark
3 having little weight; easy to lift
4 to set on fire

lighthouse

a tower with a bright light on top to warn ships of danger

a b c d e f g h i j k l L m n o p q r s t u v w x y z

a b c d e f g h i j k **l L** m n o p q r s t u v w x y z

lightning

a flash of light that you sometimes see in the sky during a storm

like

1 to be fond of
2 the same or almost the same as

lilac

1 a pale purple or white flower with a lovely scent
2 a pale purple colour

limb

an arm, a leg or a wing

limp

the way you walk if you have hurt your foot or your leg

line

1 a long thin mark
2 people or things standing one behind the other; a queue

lion

a large wild animal of the cat family

lip

one of the outer edges of the mouth

liquid

something that flows (for example, water or milk)

list

a number of names or things written down one after the other

listen

to try to hear

literacy

being able to read and write

litre (say 'leeter')

a measure of liquid (equal to 1000 millilitres)

little

small

live

1 to stay in a place
2 to be alive

load

1 to put things onto a vehicle or ship
2 something heavy that is carried

loaf

a large piece of bread that may be cut into slices

lock

to fasten something so that only a key will open it

loft

a room just under the roof of a house

log

a large piece of wood sawn off a tree

lollipop (lolly)

a sweet on the end of a stick (see also **ice lolly**)

lonely

feeling sad and alone; without friends

long

1 of great length; not short
2 to wish for something very much

look

1 to try to see
2 **look after** to care for; to make sure that another living thing has all that it needs

loop

a long thin circle made with a piece of thread, such as cotton, wool or string

loose

not tied or fixed; free to move

lord

a title given to a man by a king or queen

lorry

a large vehicle for carrying heavy things

lose

1 not to be able to find something
2 to be beaten; not to win

loud

making a lot of noise

love

to like very much

a
b
c
d
e
f
g
h
i
j
k
l
m M
n
o
p
q
r
s
t
u
v
w
x
y
z

lovely

beautiful

low

not high; near to the ground; close to the bottom of something

luck

chance

lucky

having good luck

lump

1   a swelling
2   a piece of something

lunch

a meal eaten in the middle of the day

lung

part of the body with which you breathe (you have two lungs)

lying

saying things that are not true; telling lies

m M

machine

something made out of many parts that work together to do a job

machinery

machines; parts of a machine

mackerel

a kind of sea fish used as a food

mad

1   crazy; very foolish
2   very angry

magazine

a thin book with things to read and many photos; it comes out once a week or once a month

magic

strange and wonderful things that happen

magician

a person who performs magic tricks or makes wonderful things happen

magnet

a piece of iron or steel that attracts other pieces of iron or steel

mail

letters and parcels sent by post

main

most important

make

1 to build; to put things together to make something new
2 to force someone to do something

male

a person or an animal that can one day be a father; a man or boy

man men

a grown-up male person

manage

to be able to do something

many

a lot of

map

a drawing that helps you find your way around a place

marble

a small round ball made of glass or stone and used as a toy

march

to walk with others, sometimes to music

a b c d e f g h i j k l m M n o p q r s t u v w x y z

a
b
c
d
e
f
g
h
i
j
k
l

m M

n
o
p
q
r
s
t
u
v
w
x
y
z

margarine

a food made from vegetable oils, often used instead of butter

mark

1 a sign put on something
2 a spot that has been put on something by mistake
3 to put a mark on

market

a place where goods are bought and sold

marry

to start being someone's husband or wife

marvellous

wonderful

mask

a covering for the face

mass

how heavy something is

mast

the tall pole used to hold up the sails on a ship

mat

a small rug

match matches

1 a small stick with a tip that catches fire easily
2 a game between two teams

material

1 anything from which things can be made
2 cloth

meal

the food you eat at a certain time of day (for example, lunch)

mean

selfish

measure

to find out how long or heavy something is

meat

the main part of an animal
that is used as food

medicine

something you take to make
you better when you are ill

meet

1 to come together
2 to be in the same place as
   someone so that you can talk

melt

to turn into liquid
because of heat

memory

1 the part of the brain with
   which you remember
2 a thought about the past

mend

to put right; to repair

menu

a list of things you can eat
in a restaurant

mess

things mixed together
in an untidy way

message

news sent from one person
to another

metal

materials such as iron, steel,
gold, silver and brass

metre (say 'meeter')

a measure of length equal
to 100 centimetres

microphone

something you use to make
your voice sound louder
or to record your voice

microwave

a special kind of electronic
oven that cooks food quickly

midday

12 o'clock in the day; noon

middle

the part of something that
is the same distance from
each end or side

a
b
c
d
e
f
g
h
i
j
k
l
m M
n
o
p
q
r
s
t
u
v
w
x
y
z

a
b
c
d
e
f
g
h
i
j
k
l

m M

n
o
p
q
r
s
t
u
v
w
x
y
z

midnight

12 o'clock at night

mile

a measure of distance

milk

a white liquid produced by mothers and some female animals to feed their babies

milkshake

a drink made from milk, sometimes with a special taste (strawberry or chocolate, for example)

mill

1   a place where grain is made into flour
2   a kind of factory
3   a small machine for making things into a fine powder (for example, pepper or salt)

millennium

1000 years

mime

to use movements instead of words to say something or to tell a story

mince

to chop up very small

mind

1   to look after
2   a person's way of thinking

mineral

a material such as rock that is dug out of the earth

minibus

a small bus with lots of seats for carrying people

mint

1   a plant used to flavour food
2   a sweet flavoured with mint

minute

a length of time of 60 seconds; there are 60 minutes in one hour

miracle

a strange and wonderful event

mirror

a piece of glass in which you can see yourself

miserable

full of sadness

miss

not to see or find

Miss

a title given to a woman or girl who is not married

mistake

something you have done that is wrong

mix

to put things together

mixture

things mixed together

mobile phone (mobile)

a phone that you can use almost anywhere

model

1 a small copy of something
2 a pattern to be followed
3 a person who shows off clothes

moment

a very short space of time

money

the coins and notes that you use when buying and selling things

monkey

an animal with a long tail; it has hands and feet a bit like ours

monster

a large frightening creature that you read about in stories

month

one of the 12 parts of the year

mood

the way you feel

moon

the round object that goes around the earth and can be seen in the sky at night

a
b
c
d
e
f
g
h
i
j
k
l
m M
n
o
p
q
r
s
t
u
v
w
x
y
z

a
b
c
d
e
f
g
h
i
j
k
l
m M
n
o
p
q
r
s
t
u
v
w
x
y
z

mop

soft material at the end of a long pole, used for cleaning

morning

the part of the day before noon

mosque (say 'mosk')

a place where Muslims worship

moss

a furry green plant that grows on wet ground, stones and trees

moth

an insect like a butterfly that usually flies at night

mother (mummy, mum)

a female parent

motor

a machine that makes things move

motorway

a wide road where vehicles can go fast

mountain

a very large and steep hill

mouse mice

1 a small animal with a long tail
2 a small piece of equipment that you use to move the pointer on a computer

moustache

hair growing on the top lip

mouth

the part of the face with which you speak, eat and drink

move

to go or take from one place to another

movement

what happens when someone or something moves

movie

a film; a story shown in a cinema

mow

to cut grass

Mr (say 'mister')

title given to a man

Mrs (say 'missiz')

title given to a married woman

Ms (say 'miz')

title given to a woman who may or may not be married

mud

wet earth

muddle

a mess or a mix-up

mug

a big cup, usually with straight sides

multiply

to add the same number many times (×)

Mummy (Mum)

a name for your mother

mumps

a painful illness that gives you a sore neck and throat

munch

to eat noisily

murmur

to speak very quietly

muscle

one of the parts of the body that you use to move

museum

a building where old and interesting things can be seen

mushroom mushrooms

a kind of plant shaped like a small umbrella; some mushrooms can be eaten but others are poisonous

music

pleasant sounds made by people singing or playing instruments

musical

to do with music

mutter

to speak or complain in a quiet voice

mystery

something strange that cannot be explained

m M

a
b
c
d
e
f
g
h
i
j
k
l
n
o
p
q
r
s
t
u
v
w
x
y
z

nN

nail nails

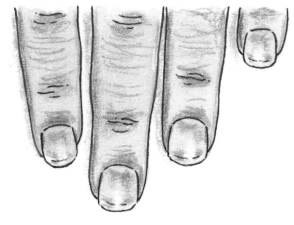

1 the hard shiny covering on the end of a finger or toe

2 a small pointed piece of metal used to join pieces of wood together

name

what you call someone or something

narrow

not far across; not wide

nasty

not pleasant; not good to taste

nature

everything in the world not made by people (for example, the weather, animals, plants and rocks)

naughty (say 'norty')

badly behaved

near

close to

nearly

almost

neat

tidy; done carefully

neck

the part of the body joining the head and the shoulders

necklace

a string of beads or jewels worn round the neck

need

to want badly

needle

a piece of metal with a sharp point at one end; some needles have a hole in them and are used for sewing

neighbour

a person who lives next door or quite near

nephew

a son of a brother or a sister

nervous

afraid; easily frightened or worried

nest

a place used as a home by birds and some animals

net

1 threads of string or wire, twisted together; a net lets small objects through but catches larger ones
2 see **internet**

nettle

a wild plant that stings when touched

new

just made or bought; not used or known before

news

information about something that has just happened

newspaper (paper)

sheets of paper printed every day or every week to give news

next

1 nearest
2 following

nice

pleasant

niece

a daughter of a brother or a sister

a
b
c
d
e
f
g
h
i
j
k
l
m
n **N**
o
p
q
r
s
t
u
v
w
x
y
z

a
b
c
d
e
f
g
h
i
j
k
l
m
n N
o
p
q
r
s
t
u
v
w
x
y
z

night

the time of day when it is dark

nightdress (nightie)

a loose kind of dress worn in bed by girls and women

nightmare

a bad or frightening dream

nimble

quick and light on your feet

nip

to bite; to pinch

nod

to bend your head forward quickly

noise

a sound, often loud and unpleasant

non-fiction

something that tells you about real things (for example, real people, real places or things that have really happened)

nonsense

words that do not make sense

noodles

very long thin strips of pasta, often used in Chinese cooking

noon

12 o'clock in the day; midday

north

the direction that is on the left as you face the rising sun

nose

the part of your face that you use to breathe and to smell things through

note

1 a short letter
2 a single sound in music
3 a piece of paper money; a bank note

notice

1 to see something
2 a piece of paper stuck to a wall; a sign that tells you something

now

at this moment

oO

nuisance
something that annoys you or makes things difficult for you

number
a word or figure that tells you how many (for example, one, two, three, 1, 2, 3)

numeracy
being able to work with numbers

nurse

a person trained to look after sick people and to help you to keep well

nursery
1 a place where young children are looked after and can play and learn
2 a place where young plants are grown

nut nuts

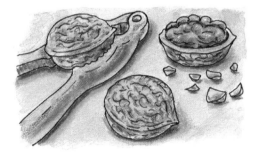

the seed of a tree; it has a hard shell

oak
a large tree with fruits called acorns

oar oars

a pole with a flat end, used to move a boat through water

obey
to do as you are told

object
something that you can see or touch

oblong
a shape like a square but with two sides longer than the other two, like this page

ocean
a very large sea

a b c d e f g h i j k l m n o **O** p q r s t u v w x y z

a
b
c
d
e
f
g
h
i
j
k
l
m
n
o O
p
q
r
s
t
u
v
w
x
y
z

octopus

a sea creature with
eight long arms

odd

1 not even (for example, 1, 3
   and 5 are odd numbers)
2 strange

off

1 when something is not
   working; the opposite of **on**
2 when food has gone bad

offer

1 to hold something out
   for someone to take
2 to say that you are ready
   to do something or
   ready to give something
   to another person

office

a place where people work,
usually at desks

officer

a person who is in charge
and must decide things

often

many times

oil

a smooth and greasy liquid

old

1 bought, made or born a long
   time ago; not new or young
2 having lived for a certain
   number of years
3 **old fashioned** like something
   from a long time ago

on

1 when something is working;
   the opposite of **off**
2 when something is placed
   on top of something else

once

1 one time
2 in the past

onion

a round vegetable with a
very strong smell and taste

only

1 alone
2 no more than

open

not shut; not covered over

opposite

1 the side facing you
2 as different as possible

orange

1 a round fruit with lots
  of juice that is grown in
  some hot countries
2 the colour of this fruit

orchestra

a large group of people
playing different musical
instruments together

order

1 to say what must be done or
  what things you want to buy
2 neatly arranged things
  or ideas

out

1 not inside
2 away from home
3 not lit; not burning

outside

not inside; not in a building
or room

oval

egg-shaped

oven

a kind of box that can be
heated for cooking or baking

over

1 above
2 finished
3 more than
4 across

owl

a bird with large eyes
that hunts at night

own

1 to have
2 belonging to yourself

a
b
c
d
e
f
g
h
i
j
k
l
m
n
o O
p
q
r
s
t
u
v
w
x
y
z

a
b
c
d
e
f
g
h
i
j
k
l
m
n
o
p P
q
r
s
t
u
v
w
x
y
z

pP

page

one side of a piece of paper in a book, newspaper or magazine

pain

the unpleasant feeling you get when you are hurt or when you are ill

paint

1   to put paint on something; to make a picture
2   a coloured liquid used to cover something

painting

a picture that is painted

pair

two things of the same kind; a set of two

palace

a large building lived in by an important person (for example, a king or a queen)

pack

1   to put things into a box, parcel or suitcase
2   a group of things such as animals or playing cards

packet

a small box or container made of paper or cardboard

pad

1   several sheets of paper stuck together at the top edge
2   something soft and thick that is used to clean or protect things

paddle

1   to walk and splash around in shallow water for fun
2   a long piece of wood with a wide flat end, used to move a canoe or small boat

pale

with little colour

pan

a round metal pot with a long handle, used for cooking

pancake

a thin cake of flour, eggs and milk, fried in a pan

panda

a black and white animal like a small bear

pant

to breathe quickly with an open mouth, especially after running

pantomime

a fairy story performed on the stage with music and songs

pants

see **underpants**

paper

1 material for writing, printing, drawing or painting on
2 a newspaper

parcel

something wrapped up for posting or carrying

parent

a father or mother

park

1 a piece of land where you can go to play, walk or enjoy yourself; it usually has grass and flowers
2 to leave a vehicle somewhere for a time

parrot

a bird that has brightly-coloured feathers and a curved beak

part

one piece of a whole thing

partner

one of two people who do something together (for example, play a game, work together, live together, dance together)

a b c d e f g h i j k l m n o **p P** q r s t u v w x y z

a b c d e f g h i j k l m n o **p P** q r s t u v w x y z

party

a group of people who have got together to enjoy themselves

pass

1 to leave behind; to go past
2 to get through a test

passenger

someone who is travelling in a vehicle but is not driving it

past

1 the time that has gone
2 up to and away from

pasta

an Italian food that comes in many different shapes

paste

a wet and sticky mixture that can be spread easily

pastry

a mixture of flour, water and fat, used for baking pies and tarts

pat

to touch gently with the hand

patch

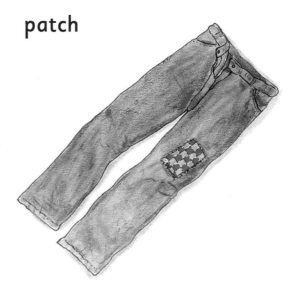

a small piece of material used to repair a hole

path

a narrow track for walking

patient

1 able to wait calmly
2 someone who is ill and seeing a doctor or dentist

pattern

1 lines and shapes repeated to look good
2 a drawing to follow when making something

pavement

the path that you walk on beside a street

paw

the foot of an animal
such as a dog or a cat

pay

1 to hand over money
for something
2 money you are given
for working

pea

a round green seed that grows
in a pod, used as food

peace

1 quietness; stillness; calm
2 not being at war

peach

a round fruit with lots of
juice, a soft furry skin and a
large and hard seed inside

peacock

a large male bird with a
beautiful tail shaped like a fan;
the female is called a peahen

pear

a soft yellow or green fruit
with lots of juice and a
rounded shape that gets
narrow at the top

pedal

the part of a bike that you
push on with your feet

peel

1 the outside skin of fruit
or vegetables
2 to take off the outer covering

peg

1 a curved piece of metal or
plastic for hanging clothes on
2 a little piece of wood
or plastic with a spring
inside, for fixing clothes
to a washing line

pen

a writing tool containing ink

pence

plural of penny

pencil

a writing tool made of wood
with a coloured or grey centre

penguin

a large black and white sea bird
that lives in very cold places;
it cannot fly but it can swim

penny pennies or pence

a small British coin; there
are 100 pence in a pound

a b c d e f g h i j k l m n o p P q r s t u v w x y z

a
b
c
d
e
f
g
h
i
j
k
l
m
n
o

p P

q
r
s
t
u
v
w
x
y
z

people

men, women and children

pepper

1 a pale powder, often used with salt to flavour food
2 a hollow vegetable that can be red, yellow or green

perform

to do something, sometimes in front of an audience

pet

an animal that you look after at home

petal

one of the parts of a flower

photocopier

a machine for making a photocopy

photocopy

1 to make a copy of something using a photocopier
2 a copy made using a photocopier

photograph (photo)

a picture taken using a camera

piano

a large musical instrument with black and white keys

pie

fruit or meat cooked in pastry

piece

a part of something larger

pig

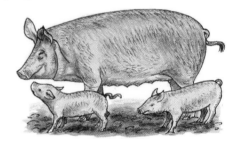

an animal kept on a farm; pork and bacon are made from pigs

pigeon

a fat grey bird that makes soft noises and is often seen in towns

pile

a heap

pillow

a cushion to rest your head on in bed

pilot

a person who flies a plane

pimple

a small spot on the skin

pin

a tiny piece of pointed metal that is thin and sharp; pins are used for holding things together

pinch

1 to nip tightly with the fingers
2 a very small amount

pineapple

a large fruit with lots of juice, grown in some hot countries

pink

a very light red colour

pint

a measure of liquids (the same as about half a litre)

pip

a small seed

pipe

a tube that can carry a gas or liquid from one place to another

pirate

a sea robber

pit

a hole in the ground

pitch

an area of ground for playing games on

pizza (say 'peetsa')

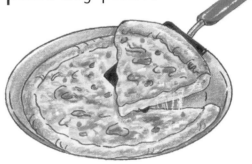

a flat open pie, topped with cheese, tomatoes or other foods and eaten hot

place

a space for something

plane

see aeroplane

plant

1 something that grows in soil
2 to put something into the soil to grow

a b c d e f g h i j k l m n o p P q r s t u v w x y z

a
b
c
d
e
f
g
h
i
j
k
l
m
n
o
p P
q
r
s
t
u
v
w
x
y
z

plaster

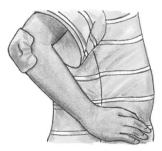

a strip of sticky material that you put over a cut on your skin

plastic

a light and strong material used to make many different objects

play

1 to do something for fun (for example, sports or games)
2 to make music with an instrument (for example, a piano)
3 a story that is acted

playground

a place for children to play, often with swings and slides

pleasant

nice, pleasing, making you happy

please

1 to make someone happy
2 the word you use when you ask for something

plural

more than one

pocket

a bag sewn into clothes to hold money and other things

pod

in some plants, this is the part that contains the seeds

poem

a piece of poetry

poet

a person who writes poems

poetry

words written in lines of a certain length and often rhyming at the end

point

1 to show with a finger
2 the sharp end
3 a dot

poison

something that can harm or kill you if it gets into your body

poisonous

containing poison

pole

a long rounded stick

police

people who make sure that the law is obeyed

police car

a special car that a police officer drives

polish

1 to make something smooth and bright by rubbing
2 a powder, wax or liquid used for polishing

polite

well behaved; not rude

pond

a small lake

pony

a small horse

pool

1 a place for playing or swimming in water
2 a small pond

poor

1 not having much money; not rich
2 not very good

popcorn

a snack made of corn with salt or sugar; it is often eaten at the cinema

poppadom

a thin round piece of dough, fried in oil

poppy

a wild plant with large flowers, often red

popular

well liked by people

port

a place where ships take on and drop off their cargo

possible

able to be done; may take place

a b c d e f g h i j k l m n o **p P** q r s t u v w x y z

post

1 a thick upright pole fixed in the ground
2 sending and receiving letters

postcard

Hi Winston,
Having a good time by the sea.
I learned to swim.
Love Ella

Winston Green
2 Park Street
Redtown Hill
Oxford

a card with a photo on it, which you send when you are on holiday

poster

a large piece of paper with a message on it, which is put up in a public place

postman, postwoman

the person who collects and delivers your mail

pot

a deep round container; some pots are used for cooking

potato

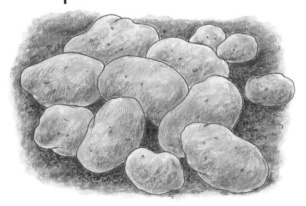

an oval or round vegetable grown under the ground

pound

1 an amount of British money equal to 100 pence (£)
2 a measure of weight

pour

1 to make liquid flow out of a container
2 to rain heavily

powder

tiny pieces made by crushing a hard material

practice

doing something often so that you get better at it

practise

to do something often so that you get better at it

pray

to speak to God

precious

very valuable; much loved

pre-school

where children can go to
learn and play when they
are three years old

present

a gift

preserve

to keep something from
harm or from going bad

press

to push hard

pretend

1 to act as though you were
   somebody or something else
2 to act as though something
   is true when it is not

pretty

pleasant to see; looking nice

price

what you must pay to buy
something; the cost

prick

to make a small hole with
something pointed

priest

a person whose job it
is to run a church

primrose

a small wild plant that has
yellow flowers in spring

prince

a man or boy in a royal family

princess

a woman or girl in a
royal family

print

1 to press letters onto
   paper using a machine
2 to write without joining
   up the letters

printer

1 a machine that prints things
2 a person who operates
   a printing machine

a
b
c
d
e
f
g
h
i
j
k
l
m
n
o
p P
q
r
s
t
u
v
w
x
y
z

prison

a place where people who have broken the law are kept

prisoner

a person who has been sent to prison

private

belonging to one person or group only

prize

a reward given if you are very good at something or if you are lucky

problem

a difficult thing to work out

program

instruction that tells a computer what to do

programme

information about what will happen (at a play or a concert, for example)

promise

to say that you really will do something

protect

to stop someone or something from being harmed or damaged

proud

being very pleased with someone or something because it is very good

prove

to show that something is true

public

for everybody to use

pudding

something sweet that you eat at the end of a meal

puddle

a very small pool (of rain water, for example)

puffin

a sea bird with a short thick beak

pull

to drag something towards you

puncture

a small hole made by
something pointed

punish

to make someone unhappy
because they have done
something wrong

pupil

a person who is being taught,
especially in a school

puppet

a kind of doll that can be made
to move by pulling strings or
by putting your hand inside

puppy

a young dog

purple

a colour made by mixing
red and blue

purse

a small bag for holding money

push

to press against something
to try to move it

pushchair

a chair on wheels in which you
push a baby or small child

put

to place something

puzzle

1 something that is
   difficult to understand
2 a game that has to
   be worked out

pyjamas

trousers and a top worn in bed

pylon pylons

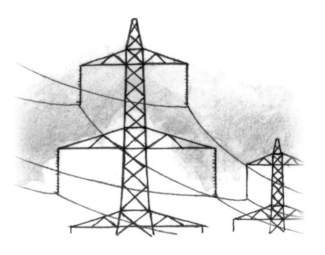

a large metal tower that
supports cables high up
in the air

pyramid

a shape or building that has a
flat bottom and sides that are
triangles which meet in a point

a
b
c
d
e
f
g
h
i
j
k
l
m
n
o
p P
q
r
s
t
u
v
w
x
y
z

a
b
c
d
e
f
g
h
i
j
k
l
m
n
o
p
q Q
r
s
t
u
v
w
x
y
z

qQ

When you see the letters 'qu' at the beginning of a word, you usually say 'kw'.

quack

the noise made by ducks

quantity

an amount

quarrel

to disagree angrily with someone

quarry

a place where stone is taken out of the ground

quarter

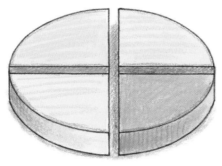

one of the four equal parts of something

queen

1 a woman who is the ruler of a country
2 the wife of a king

question

something that needs an answer

queue (here you say 'Q')

a line of waiting people or vehicles

quick

fast; at great speed

quiet

with very little or no sound; not loud

quilt

a thick cover for a bed

quite

1 completely; fully
2 a little, but not very much

quiz

a game in which questions have to be answered

rabbit

a small furry animal that
lives in a hole in the ground

race

1   a test of speed
2   people of the same kind

racket

1   a kind of bat, but with
    strings instead of flat wood
    (used in tennis, for example)
2   a lot of very loud noise

radio

a piece of equipment that
receives special waves;
these waves are turned into
sounds for you to listen to

raft

a flat boat, often made
of logs tied together

rag

a piece of cloth that is
old or torn

rage

great anger; a strong temper

rail

a fixed wooden, plastic
or metal bar

railway

everything to do with trains

rain

drops of water falling
from the clouds

rainbow

curved stripes of different
colours, seen in the sky when
the sun shines through rain

raise

1   to lift up
2   to look after any living
    creature from the time
    when it is very young

a
b
c
d
e
f
g
h
i
j
k
l
m
n
o
p
q
r R
s
t
u
v
w
x
y
z

a b c d e f g h i j k l m n o p q **r R** s t u v w x y z

raisin

a dried grape

Ramadan

an important Muslim festival

raspberry

a small dark red berry
with lots of juice

rat

an animal like a large mouse

rattle

1 the noise of things being
   shaken together
2 a baby's toy that you shake

raw

not cooked

reach

1 to stretch and touch
2 to arrive at; to get to

read

to understand the meaning
of written or printed words

ready

1 willing to do something
2 can be used straight away
   because everything
   needed has been done

real

true; not false

reason

why something happens; how
something can be explained

receive

to take; to get something
that is given or sent

recent

just happened

recipe

a list of instructions telling
you how to cook something

record (say 'record')

1 the best that has been
   done so far
2 something written down to
   tell you what has happened

record (say 'record')

1 to put voices or music
   onto a disk so that you
   can listen to them again
2 to write down

recorder

a wooden or plastic musical instrument played by blowing

recycle

to separate your rubbish so that some of it (glass or paper, for example) can be used again to make new things

red

the colour of blood

referee

the person who makes sure that a game is played fairly and that the players obey the rules

refrigerator (fridge)

a special kind of container for keeping food cold

reindeer

a kind of deer with long horns, which lives in cold countries

reins

straps used to control and guide an animal (or sometimes a small child)

relation

someone in the same family

religion

a way of believing in a god

remain

to stay; not to go

remember

to bring back into the mind; not to forget

remind

to make someone remember

remove

1 to take away
2 to move from one place to another

rent

the money you pay to use something that belongs to someone else

repair

to mend; to put right

repeat

to do or say something again

reply

to answer

a
b
c
d
e
f
g
h
i
j
k
l
m
n
o
p
q
r R
s
t
u
v
w
x
y
z

report

a description of something that has happened

rescue

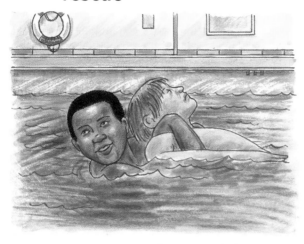

to save; to take out of danger

reservoir

a large lake that has been specially made to supply a town or city with water

rest

1 the others; what is left
2 to be still; not to work or do anything that makes you tired

restaurant

a place where you can buy and eat a meal

result

1 what happens because of something else
2 the final score in a game

return

1 to go or come back to a place
2 to give back

reward

something you are given for something good or brave you have done

rhinoceros

a large animal with one or two horns on its nose

rhyme

1 word endings that sound alike
2 a short poem with rhymes in it

rhythm

the steady beat or sound pattern of poetry or music

rib

one of the curved bones that go across your chest

ribbon

a narrow piece of material

rice

a plant grown in some hot countries; you can cook and eat the seeds

rich

having a lot of money or other valuable things

riddle

1 a word puzzle
2 a question that has a funny answer, like a joke

ride

to move about in a vehicle or on an animal

ridiculous

so silly that it might make you laugh

right

1 correct; not wrong
2 good; true
3 the opposite of left

ring

1 a circle
2 the sound made by a bell
3 a circle of metal worn on the finger

rinse

to wash with clean water, usually after washing with soap

ripe

fully grown; ready to eat

rise

1 to get up
2 to go higher

risk

the danger of something going wrong

river

a long and wide stream of water, usually flowing into the sea

road

a wide hard track on which vehicles can travel

roar

a loud and deep sound (for example, the sound a lion makes)

roast

to cook in fat in an oven or over a fire

rob

to take something that does not belong to you; to steal from

robber

a person who steals

a b c d e f g h i j k l m n o p q **r R** s t u v w x y z

robin

a small brown bird
with a red front

robot

a machine that can do some of
the work that a person can do

rock

1 stone; a large piece of stone
2 to move from side to side
3 a long and sticky sweet
that is shaped like a stick

rocket

1 a kind of firework
2 a spaceship
3 a vegetable used in salads

rod

a thin bar of wood or metal

roll

1 to turn over and over
2 something rolled into
a cylinder shape
3 a long sound made by drums
4 a kind of bread made from
small pieces of dough

roller blade, roller skate

a boot or shoe with wheels
on it, to help you move
quickly over smooth ground

roof

the top covering of a building

room

1 a part of a building with its
own floor, walls and ceiling
2 space for something

root

the part of a plant that is in
the soil and takes in water
to feed the plant

rope

a thick cord

rose

a plant with flowers
that smell very nice

rotten

1 gone bad
2 nasty; unpleasant

rough

1 not smooth
2 wild and stormy

round

the same shape as a ball or ring

rounders

a game played by two sides with a bat and ball

row (sounds like 'low')

1 a line of people or things
2 to move a boat using oars

row (sounds like 'now')

a noisy quarrel

rowing boat

a boat that is moved using oars

royal

to do with kings and queens

rub

to move one thing against another many times

rubber

1 a stretchy material made from rubber trees
2 a small piece of rubber used for getting rid of marks on paper (also called an **eraser**)

rubbish

1 things that are of no use; waste
2 nonsense

rude

not polite

rug

1 a small carpet; a mat
2 a kind of blanket

rugby

a game played with an oval ball that may be kicked or carried

ruin

1 a building that has fallen down
2 to wreck; to spoil

rule

1 a law that must be followed
2 to be able to tell other people what to do

a b c d e f g h i j k l m n o p q r R s t u v w x y z

a b c d e f g h i j k l m n o p q r s S t u v w x y z

ruler

1 a person whose job it is to tell other people what to do (for example, a king is a ruler)
2 a strip of wood, plastic or other material, used for measuring or drawing straight lines

rumble

a deep roll of sound like the sound of thunder

rumour

something you hear that may or may not be true

run

1 to move very quickly on foot
2 to flow

rung

a step on a ladder

rush

to move very quickly; to hurry

rust

a reddish-brown substance sometimes found on iron and steel

Ss

sack

1 a very large and strong bag
2 to remove somebody from a job

sacrifice

the giving up of something that you like very much

sad

unhappy; miserable

saddle

the seat of a bicycle; a seat for the rider of a horse

safari park

a park where you can see wild animals wandering about

safe

1 not in danger
2 a strong metal box that may be locked, for keeping valuable things in

sail

1 a large piece of strong cloth fixed onto a sailing boat; wind fills the sail and moves the boat
2 to travel in a boat

sailor

1 a person who works on a ship
2 a person who sails a yacht

salad

a dish of vegetables eaten cold and usually raw

sale

1 the selling of things
2 a time when things are sold at a lower price than usual

salt

a white mineral that is made into powder and used to flavour or preserve food

salwar kameez

loose trousers and a straight top, worn by some Asian women

same

not different

sand

powdered rock or shells often found at the seaside or in the desert

sandal

a shoe with an open top, fastened with straps

sandwich

two slices of bread with a filling between them

sari

a type of dress worn by some Asian women, made of a long piece of material that is wrapped around the body

a b c d e f g h i j k l m n o p q r s **S** t u v w x y z

a
b
c
d
e
f
g
h
i
j
k
l
m
n
o
p
q
r
s **S**
t
u
v
w
x
y
z

satellite

an object moving in space round another object (for example, the moon is the earth's satellite)

sauce

a thick liquid eaten with other food to add flavour

sausage sausages

minced meat in a thin skin

save

1 to bring a person out of danger; to rescue
2 to keep something for later

saw

1 a metal tool with sharp pointed teeth for cutting
2 to cut something with a saw (for example, wood)

say

to speak

scale

1 a set of numbers or marks for measuring
2 a set of musical notes going up and down
3 a small piece of flat shiny material (on the skin of a fish or snake, for example)

scales

a machine for weighing people or things

scar

a mark left on the skin by a wound

scarce

not often found because there are not many of them

scare

to frighten

scarf

a length of cloth used as a covering for the neck, shoulders or head

scatter

to throw something about in different directions

scene

1 a view
2 a part of a play
3 the place where something happened

scent

1 a pleasant smell
2 the smell that an animal leaves behind it

school

a place where people, usually children, go to learn

science

the facts about nature and how things are made

scientist

a person who studies science

scissors

a cutting tool with two knives joined together in the middle

scooter

1 a board with two wheels and a long handle; you put one foot on the board, hold on to the handle and push yourself forward with the other foot
2 a small motorbike

score

1 to count points or goals in a game or competition
2 the number of points or goals scored in a game or competition

scrap

1 a tiny piece
2 rubbish thrown away

scrape

to rub and clean with something hard

scratch

1 to mark with something pointed or sharp
2 to rub the skin because it is itchy

scream

to make a shrill cry, usually because of fear or pain

screw

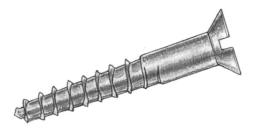

a sharp piece of metal that you turn round and round to fix things together

scribble

to write quickly and carelessly

scrub

to clean with water, and usually a brush

a b c d e f g h i j k l m n o p q r s **S** t u v w x y z

sculpture

a shape made out of stone, metal or other materials

sea

the salt water that covers much of the earth's surface

seal

a kind of sea animal with fur

search

to look very hard for something

seaside

the area of land that is right beside the sea

season

one of the four main times of the year: spring, summer, autumn or winter

seat

something to sit on

seat belt

a belt you wear in a car, coach or plane to stop you being thrown about if there is an accident

second

1 a very short length of time (there are 60 seconds in one minute)
2 after the first

secret

something known about by only a few people

see

1 what you are able to do with your eyes
2 to understand

seed seeds

a grain from which a plant grows

seek

to search for; to look for

seem

to appear to be

seesaw

a playground toy; one child sits on each end of a piece of wood and they take it in turns to go up and down

selfish

thinking only about yourself

sell

to give something to someone else, who gives you money for it

send

to make something or someone go somewhere

sense

1 smell, sight, hearing, taste or touch
2 knowing the right thing to do

sensible

having good sense

sentence

a group of words that make sense together

separate

1 not joined in any way
2 to take things to pieces so they are not together any more

serial

a story told or written in parts

serious

1 very important
2 worrying or bad
3 not laughing or smiling very much

serve

to do things for other people (for example, to help them to buy things in a shop, or to give them food and drink)

service

1 something you do for others
2 something people can use to help them (for example, a bus service)
3 a special time in church, when people pray and sing together

set

1 to put something somewhere or to get it ready
2 a group of people or things that are alike in some way
3 what happens when some liquids cool and go solid

a
b
c
d
e
f
g
h
i
j
k
l
m
n
o
p
q
r
s S
t
u
v
w
x
y
z

settee

a soft seat made for more than one person; a couch, a sofa

settle

1 to sink to the bottom
2 to calm down; to be still

sew (say 'so')

to join together with stitches using a needle and thread

shade

1 a place where there is shelter from the sun or other strong light
2 how light or dark a colour is

shadow

a dark shape seen on a surface when something keeps out the light; a dark place

shaft

something long and straight

shake

to move quickly from side to side; to shiver

shallow

not deep

shampoo

a special liquid soap that you use for washing your hair

shape

the outline of something

share

1 to divide into parts
2 to use something with someone else

shark

a large fish with sharp teeth

sharp

1 pointed; able to cut
2 quick; sudden
3 able to think, see or hear well and quickly
4 a sound that is just above the correct note in music

shave

to remove hair from the skin with a razor

shears

a tool like a big pair of scissors, used in the garden

shed

1 a small building
2 to take off, or let something fall off

sheep

a farm animal with a woolly coat

sheet

1 a large piece of cloth, often used on a bed
2 a thin and flat piece of material, such as paper, glass or metal

shelf

a board fixed to a wall or inside a cupboard, for putting things on

shell

1 the hard covering of a sea creature, sometimes found on the beach
2 the hard covering of an egg, a nut or a seed

shellfish

a small sea creature that has a shell

shelter

a place where you are protected from bad weather or danger

shepherd

a person who looks after sheep

shield

1 a large piece of metal or wood once used by soldiers to protect themselves
2 to protect from harm

shift

to move

shine

1 to give out light
2 to look bright; to sparkle

ship

a very large boat

shirt

a piece of clothing with sleeves and a collar, worn on the top part of the body

a
b
c
d
e
f
g
h
i
j
k
l
m
n
o
p
q
r
s **S**
t
u
v
w
x
y
z

a
b
c
d
e
f
g
h
i
j
k
l
m
n
o
p
q
r
s S
t
u
v
w
x
y
z

shiver

to shake because of cold or fear

shoal

a large group of fish of the same kind, all swimming together

shoe

a covering for the foot that is made of leather or plastic and has a hard bottom

shoelace

string used to tie your shoes or trainers

shoot

1 to fire a weapon
2 new growth on a plant

shop

1 to go to a shop to buy things
2 a place where things are sold

shopping

things that you buy in a shop

shore

the land at the edge of water (for example, beside a lake)

short

small from end to end like this girl's hair; not long; not tall

shorts

short trousers with legs that end above the knee

shoulder

the place where the arm joins the body

shout

to speak or cry out in a loud voice

shove (say 'shuv')

to push hard

show

1 to allow to see
2 something you watch for fun (on television or at the theatre)

shower

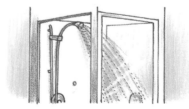

a place to wash yourself where water sprays down on you from above

shrill

very high (usually used
to describe a sound)

shrink

to get smaller

shut

1 to close
2 not open; closed

shy

afraid to speak; easily frightened

sick

1 bringing up food from
   the stomach
2 ill; not well

side

1 the part at the edge
   of something
2 the flat faces or lines between
   the corners of a shape
3 a team at games

sigh

to make a low sound
as you breathe out

sight

1 being able to see
2 something seen

sign

1 a mark, movement or
   message that tells you
   something
2 to write your name on

signal

a sign, sound or light that
tells you something

silent

quiet; still; without noise

silk

a kind of smooth soft cloth

silly

foolish; stupid

silver

a valuable grey metal,
used to make jewellery

simple

1 plain; without any patterns
2 easy

sing

to make music with the voice

a
b
c
d
e
f
g
h
i
j
k
l
m
n
o
p
q
r
s S
t
u
v
w
x
y
z

single

1 only one
2 not married

sink

1 to go down slowly,
   especially in water
2 a large fixed basin
   used for washing

sip

to drink in tiny amounts

sister sisters

a girl or woman who has the
same parents as another person

sit

to rest on your bottom
with your back upright

size

how big something is

skate

1 a metal blade fitted to a
   boot so you can move
   quickly on ice
2 to move on ice using skates
3 to move on roller skates
   or roller blades

skateboard

a board with wheels
underneath that you can
stand on and do tricks on

skeleton

all the bones in the body

ski

1 a long thin piece of wood,
   metal or plastic fitted to
   a boot so that you can
   move quickly over snow
2 to move on snow using skis

skid

to slide out of control
on a slippery surface

skill

being able to do something well

skin

the outer covering of a person,
an animal, a fruit or a vegetable

skip

1 to jump over a turning rope
2 to move with little
   jumping steps
3 a huge container for putting
   rubbish in

skirt

a piece of clothing that hangs from the waist and is worn by girls and women

skull

the bones that cover your head

sky

the place above the earth where you see the sun, moon and stars

skyscraper

a very tall building

slam

to bang; to shut loudly

slap

to hit something or someone with the flat part of your hand

slate

1 a kind of grey rock that divides easily into thin pieces
2 a piece of this, used with others to make a roof

sledge

a small vehicle without wheels, specially made to slide smoothly over snow

sleep

to rest your whole body with your eyes closed and without being conscious

sleeve

the part of a piece of clothing that covers an arm

slice

a thin piece that is cut from something larger

slide

1 a smooth surface made specially for sliding down, often found in playgrounds
2 to move smoothly on a slippery surface; to slip

sling

a bandage to support a broken arm

slip

1 to move quickly and quietly
2 to lose your balance on a smooth surface

a
b
c
d
e
f
g
h
i
j
k
l
m
n
o
p
q
r
s S
t
u
v
w
x
y
z

slippers

light soft shoes worn indoors

slippery

so wet, greasy or smooth that it is difficult to hold or walk on

slope

something that is higher at one end than at the other

slow

taking a long time; not quick

sly

not to be trusted

small

little; not big

smart

1 clever; quick to understand
2 well dressed

smash

to break into many pieces

smell

1 to notice something by using your nose
2 to have a smell

smile

a happy look

smoke

the dark cloud that comes from something burning

smooth

flat; not rough

smoothie

a drink made from fruit or vegetables mixed together

smudge

a dirty mark that is usually made when you are writing

smuggle

to take things into or out of a country secretly

snack

a small amount of food
eaten between meals

snail

a small slow-moving animal
with a shell on its back

snake

a smooth animal with no
legs that glides on its body

snap

1 to bite at something quickly
2 to break with a sharp noise

snatch

to grab quickly

sneak

to move secretly

sneeze

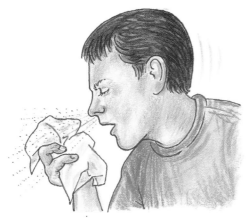

a sudden and noisy rush
of air from the nose

sniff

to smell noisily with
quick breaths

snore

to breathe heavily and
noisily while asleep

snow

frozen water that falls in
white flakes

soak

1 to make very wet
2 to leave in liquid for a time

soap

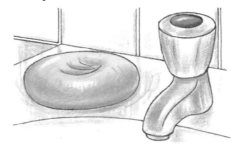

a fatty material that is used
with water for washing

sob

to weep noisily

a b c d e f g h i j k l m n o p q r s **S** t u v w x y z

a
b
c
d
e
f
g
h
i
j
k
l
m
n
o
p
q
r
s S
t
u
v
w
x
y
z

sock

a covering for your foot and ankle

sofa

a soft chair for more than one person; a couch or settee

soft

1   not hard
2   gentle; not rough
3   quiet; not loud

soil

1   the earth in which plants grow
2   to make dirty

soldier

a member of an army; a person who fights

solid

1   hard; firm; not liquid or gas
2   not hollow

solve

to find the answer to a problem

somersault

to turn head over heels

son

a male child of a parent

song

a piece of music for the voice, with words as well as a tune

soon

in a short time

sore

Mind your head

painful

sorry

feeling unhappy because of something you have done or something that has happened

sort

1   a kind; a type
2   to put into order

sound

something you hear; a noise

soup

a liquid food made by boiling vegetables, meat or fish in water

sour

having a sharp and bitter taste, like a lemon

south

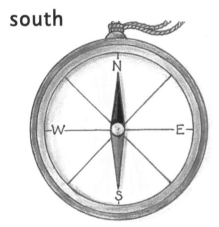

the direction that is on the right as you face the rising sun

sow (sounds like 'low')

to put seeds into the ground so that they will grow

sow (sounds like 'now')

a female pig

space

1   the distance between things
2   the place beyond the earth's atmosphere

spaceship

a vehicle made to travel in space

spade

1   a tool made for digging soil
2   one of the four kinds in a pack of playing cards

spaghetti

long strings of pasta

spare

not in use at present; extra

spark

a tiny piece of burning material

sparkle

to shine with tiny dots of light that seem to move

a b c d e f g h i j k l m n o p q r s **S** t u v w x y z

a b c d e f g h i j k l m n o p q r **s S** t u v w x y z

sparrow

a small brown bird, often seen near houses

speak

to use the voice to say something; to talk

spear

a weapon with a long thin handle and a sharp point

special

1 of a kind that is different
2 made or done for one person or event

speech

the sounds that you make when you speak

speed

the quickness or slowness with which something is done

spell

1 to arrange letters one by one to make words
2 magic words that make things happen in stories

spend

to give money to pay for something

spider

a small creature with eight legs that weaves a web to catch insects for food

spill

to let a liquid or powder out of its container by mistake

spin

1 to turn round and round very quickly
2 to make cotton or wool into thread

spine

the backbone

spit

1 the liquid that forms in your mouth
2 to force something out of your mouth

splash

to throw or scatter liquid noisily

splendid

1 excellent; very good
2 very grand

spoil

to ruin; to damage

sponge

1 a soft object that soaks up water, used for washing
2 a soft light cake

spoon

a tool used for eating or stirring soft foods or liquids

sport

games played for exercise or pleasure

spot spots

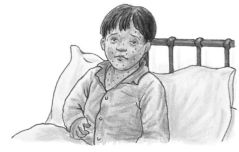

1 a tiny mark
2 to notice

spray

1 thin jets of water
2 a small bunch of flowers

spread

1 to scatter about
2 to cover a surface with something

spring

1 to jump in the air
2 a curled piece of metal that jumps back when you try to press it down
3 a place where water appears from below the ground
4 the season between winter and summer

sprinkle

to scatter in small drops or tiny pieces

sprout

to begin to grow

spy

a person who finds and passes on information secretly

square

a shape with four equal sides, like this ■

squash

to crush; to squeeze tightly together

a b c d e f g h i j k l m n o p q r s **S** t u v w x y z

a b c d e f g h i j k l m n o p q r **s S** t u v w x y z

squeak

a small sharp noise like the sound made by a mouse

squeal

a long shrill cry, often made in pain or in joy

squeeze

to press together; to squash

squirrel

a small animal with a bushy tail that lives among trees

stable

a building where horses are kept

stage

part of a room where the floor is raised so that everyone can see what is happening there

stairs

a set of steps leading to another floor in a building

stalk

the stem of a flower or plant

stall

a counter for selling things at (in a market, for example)

stamp

1 the little piece of paper stuck on a letter or parcel to show that you have paid to send it by post
2 to put your feet down hard and noisily

stand

1 to be upright
2 to rise up

star

1 one of the bright objects that can be seen in the sky on a clear night
2 a very famous person, such as an actor, a singer or a footballer

stare

to look at something steadily for a long time

starling

a noisy bird with dark shiny feathers

start

to begin

starve

to be ill or die because you have no food

station

a place where trains stop

stay

not to go away; to remain

steady

not moving; not changing; not too fast

steal

to take something that is not yours; to rob

steam

the mist or cloud that comes from boiling or very hot water

steel

a strong metal

steep

sloping sharply

steer

to make a car or some other vehicle go the way you want it to

stem

the thin part of a plant on which the leaves or flowers grow

step

1 to put one foot in front of the other when you walk or run
2 a flat place at a different level from the floor; you put your feet there to move up or down (on stairs, for example)

a b c d e f g h i j k l m n o p q r s **S** t u v w x y z

a
b
c
d
e
f
g
h
i
j
k
l
m
n
o
p
q
r

s S

t
u
v
w
x
y
z

stepfamily

the new family that comes together when a parent gets married again (for example, **stepfather**, **stepmother**, **stepbrother**, **stepsister**, **stepdaughter**, **stepson**)

stew

meat and vegetables cooked slowly in water

stick

1 a short thin piece of wood
2 to join together with glue
3 **to stick out** to be longer than the things around or beneath

sticky

something that can stick to things (jam or glue, for example)

stiff

hard; difficult to bend

still

1 not moving; quiet
2 the same now as before

sting

the sharp pain you get when an insect, an animal or a plant pricks your skin

stir

to move something round and round with a stick or a spoon

stitch

a loop of thread made in sewing or knitting

stomach (tummy)

where your food goes after you swallow it

stone

1 a hard material found on or below the surface of the earth
2 a precious jewel
3 a hard seed found in some kinds of fruit

stool

a seat without a back

stop

to end doing something

store

1 a place for keeping things
2 to save something for later
3 a large shop

storm

rough weather with
wind and rain

story

something that is told,
usually about things that
are not real; fiction

straight

1 without a bend or turning
2 **straight away** immediately

strange

odd

stranger

a person you do not know;
a person who does not know
the area

strap

a long piece of strong material
(leather, for example)

straw

1 the dry stalks of wheat
   or other grain
2 a thin tube for drinking
   through

strawberry strawberries

a kind of soft bright red fruit
that grows on small plants

stream

anything that is moving
steadily (for example, the
water in a small river)

street

a road with buildings beside it

strength

how strong someone
or something is

stretch

to make longer or wider
by pulling

stretcher

a long piece of material with
sticks down two sides, used
to carry a person who is ill
or has been hurt

strict

firm; making sure that
you obey the rules

a b c d e f g h i j k l m n o p q r s **S** t u v w x y z

a
b
c
d
e
f
g
h
i
j
k
l
m
n
o
p
q
r
s S
t
u
v
w
x
y
z

strike

1 to hit something hard
2 when workers will not work

string

thin cord used for tying things

strip

1 a long narrow piece
   of something
2 to undress; to uncover

stripes

lots of lines in different
colours, making a pattern

stroke

to move your hand gently
over something

strong

1 able to do difficult things
   with the body (able to lift
   heavy things, for example)
2 brave; not easily hurt or
   damaged

struggle

1 to fight
2 to try very hard to
   do something

stuff

to fill something very full

stupid

having no sense; silly

submarine

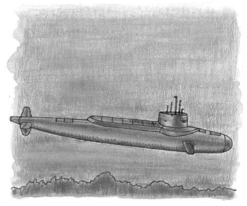

a ship that can go under water

subtract

to take one number away
from another (−)

suitcase

a container with a handle,
used for carrying clothes

sulk

to show that you are in a bad
mood by not saying anything

sum

1 a problem that you solve
   using numbers
2 the number you get
   when you add other
   numbers together

summer

the warmest season of the year, between spring and autumn

sun

the large ball of fire in the sky that gives the earth light and heat

supermarket

a large shop where people go to buy food and other things

supper

a meal eaten in the evening

support

1 to hold up from underneath
2 to help someone

suppose

to believe something to be true without knowing for sure

sure

certain; not having any doubt

surface

the top or outside of something

surgery

a place where doctors or dentists work

surname

the family name; your last name

surprise

1 something nice that you did not expect
2 the good feeling that this gives you

swallow

1 to take in through the mouth and throat
2 a kind of small bird with pointed wings and a long tail that divides in two

swan

a large white water bird with a long neck

swap

to give something away and receive something else in return

a b c d e f g h i j k l m n o p q r s S t u v w x y z

swear

to use bad words

sweat

liquid that comes through your skin when you are hot

sweatshirt

a type of jumper

sweep

to clean the floor using a brush

sweet

1 with a pleasant taste like sugar; not sour
2 a small piece of sweet food (for example, a chocolate or a toffee)
3 a dessert; a pudding

sweetcorn

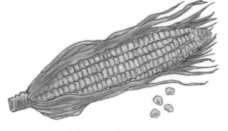

a vegetable with small bright yellow seeds

swelling

a part that becomes bigger, especially on the body

swift

1 very fast
2 a kind of small bird with long narrow wings

swim

to move in water by moving parts of the body

swing

1 a moving seat on ropes
2 a ride on a swing
3 to move backwards and forwards when hanging from something

switch

something you press to turn things on and off

sword

a metal weapon like a long knife that is sharp on two sides

synagogue

a place where Jewish people worship God

tT

table

a flat piece of furniture that stands on legs

tablet

medicine made into a small rounded shape so that it is easy to swallow

tadpole tadpoles

a small black water animal with a long tail, which grows into a frog or toad

tail

the part of a creature that sticks out at the back

take

1 to get hold of
2 to carry away

tale

a story

talk

to speak; to say something

tall

very high

tame

friendly; not wild

tank

1 a container made to hold a large amount of liquid or gas
2 a large vehicle that is used in war and is able to move over very rough ground

tanker

a ship or lorry that carries a large amount of liquid (oil, for example)

tap

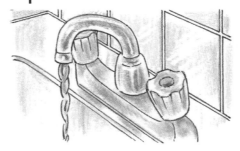

1 a knob or handle that is turned to allow liquids to flow
2 a tiny knock

a b c d e f g h i j k l m n o p q r s **t T** u v w x y z

a
b
c
d
e
f
g
h
i
j
k
l
m
n
o
p
q
r
s
t T
u
v
w
x
y
z

tape

a narrow piece of something (for example, cloth or sticky paper)

tar

a thick black liquid used to make roads

tart

a piece of pastry, usually filled with something sweet (jam or fruit, for example)

task

a piece of work that has to be done; a job

taste

1 the flavour of food or drink
2 to try a little of some food or drink

taxi

a car that will take you where you want to go; you pay the driver when you get there

tea

1 a hot drink made from the dried leaves of the tea plant
2 an evening meal

teabag

a small white see-through bag containing tea leaves; you pour boiling water onto it to make tea

teach

to help to learn

teacher

a person who teaches

team

a number of people who work or play together

tear (say 'teer')

a drop of water from the eye

tear (say 'tare')

to pull to pieces

tease

to make fun of

teddy

a soft cuddly toy in the shape of a bear

teeth

plural of **tooth**

telephone (phone)

an instrument that carries the sound of your voice by wire, using electricity

telescope

an instrument that you look through to see things that are far away

television (TV)

an instrument that makes sound and pictures from waves sent through the air

tell

to give news; to say

temper

1 the mood you are in
2 being very angry or annoyed about something

temperature

how hot or cold something is

temple

a place of worship

tennis

a game played by two or four people who use rackets to hit a ball over a net

tent

a shelter made of material that is held up by poles and ropes

term

one part of the school year

terrible

very bad

terrific

very good; excellent

a b c d e f g h i j k l m n o p q r s t **T** u v w x y z

a
b
c
d
e
f
g
h
i
j
k
l
m
n
o
p
q
r
s
t T
u
v
w
x
y
z

terrify

to frighten badly; to fill with fear

test

to try out

text

1 written words (in a story, poem or book, for example)
2 a text message that you send or receive using a mobile phone

thank

to say that you are pleased about something that someone has given to you or done for you

thaw

to melt something that was frozen (for example, snow or ice)

theatre

a building where plays are acted

theme park

a large area with lots of fairground rides

thermometer

an instrument that measures how hot or cold something is

thick

1 wide or deep; not thin
2 with a lot of things close together
3 not thin enough to flow easily

thief

a person who steals

thin

1 not fat; narrow
2 able to flow easily

think

to use the mind; to believe

thirsty

needing or wanting to drink

thought

thinking; an idea in the mind

thread

a very thin line of wool or cotton, used in sewing, knitting or weaving

throat

the front part of the neck, containing the tubes you use to breathe and swallow

throne

a special chair, usually for a king or queen

throw

to let go of something you were holding in your hand and send it through the air

thrush

a brown songbird with a spotted front

thumb

the shortest and thickest finger on your hand

thump

a heavy blow, usually made with the fist

thunder

the noisy crash that follows lightning

tick

1 a mark (✓) used to show that something has been checked or is correct
2 the sound made by a clock or a watch

ticket

a card or piece of paper allowing you to go into a special place or to travel by train, plane or bus

tickle

to touch someone lightly with your fingers to make them laugh

tide

the rising and falling of the sea each day

tidy

neat; in good order

tie

1 a narrow piece of cloth that is sometimes worn round the neck
2 to make a knot

a b c d e f g h i j k l m n o p q r s t T u v w x y z

tiger

a large and fierce animal of the cat family with black and orange striped fur

tight

fixed or fitting closely together

tights

a piece of clothing worn by girls and women to cover the feet, legs and lower part of the body

time

1 the passing of minutes, hours, days, months, seasons, years
2 the hour of the day shown on a clock

timid

easily frightened; likely to be afraid; shy

tin

a silvery-white metal

tiny

very small

tip

1 the pointed end of something
2 to upset something

tiptoe

to stand or walk on your toes

tired

needing a rest or a sleep

tissue tissues

1 a piece of soft paper for wiping (your nose, for example)
2 very thin paper used for wrapping things

title

a special name given to something or someone

toad

an animal like a large frog with a rough skin

toadstool

a kind of plant shaped like an umbrella; many toadstools are poisonous

toast

bread made crisp and brown by heat

today

this day

toe toes

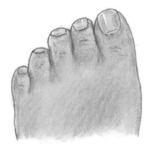

one of the five end parts of the foot

toffee

a sticky sweet made from sugar and butter

together

1 with someone or something
2 at the same time

toilet

1 a large bowl used to get rid of waste from the body
2 a room with a toilet

tomato

a soft and round red fruit, often eaten in salads

tomorrow

the day after today

tongue

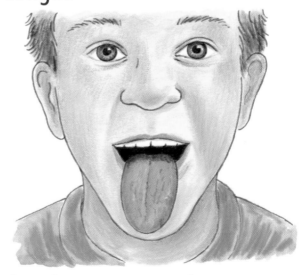

the soft moving part inside your mouth; you use it to taste, eat and speak

tonight

this night

a b c d e f g h i j k l m n o p q r s t **T** u v w x y z

a
b
c
d
e
f
g
h
i
j
k
l
m
n
o
p
q
r
s
t T
u
v
w
x
y
z

tool

an instrument that you use to do something with (for example, you use a spoon to mix things)

tooth teeth

one of the hard parts growing out of your jaw, used for biting and chewing

toothache

a pain in a tooth

toothbrush

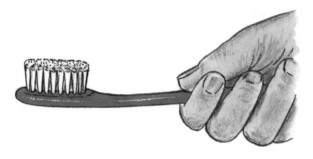

a small brush that is used to clean teeth

toothpaste

a flavoured paste that you put on your toothbrush when you clean your teeth

top

1   the highest part
2   a covering or lid for something
3   a piece of clothing worn on the top half of the body
4   a toy that spins

torch

an electric light that can be carried

tortoise

a slow-moving animal with a hard round shell

total

everything added together; the whole

touch

to feel gently with the hand or another part of the body

tough

hard; strong; not easy to cut or bite

towards

in the direction of

towel

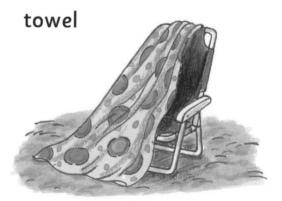

a piece of cloth for drying wet things

tower

a tall narrow building or part of a building

town

a large number of houses and other buildings grouped together

toy

something you play with

track

1 a path
2 the metal lines on which a train runs
3 a mark left in the ground (by a foot or a tyre, for example)

tractor

a strong machine for pulling heavy things

traffic

movement of vehicles and people

traffic lights

a set of coloured lights (red, orange, green) on a post where two roads cross; the lights tell the traffic when to stop or go

trail

1 to follow the track or the scent of an animal
2 to drag or be dragged behind

trailer

a cart or box on wheels, pulled by a car or lorry

train

1 railway coaches joined to an engine
2 the back part of a dress that trails on the ground
3 to teach someone to do something; to guide

trainer

a kind of shoe, often worn for sports

training

a lesson; a time when you practise something or when someone teaches you how to do something

tramp

1 a person with no home or job, who wanders around the streets
2 to walk heavily

trample

to walk heavily on, often doing damage

a b c d e f g h i j k l m n o p q r s t **T** u v w x y z

a b c d e f g h i j k l m n o p q r s t **T** u v w x y z

trampoline

a large frame with springs covered with material on which you can bounce up and down

transport

to move things or people from place to place

trap

to catch in a clever way

travel

to move from one place to another

tray

a flat piece of wood, plastic or metal, used for carrying things

treasure

something very valuable

treat

something especially pleasant that you are given

tree

a large plant with a trunk, branches and leaves

tremble

to shiver; to shake (when you are excited, frightened or cold, for example)

triangle

1 a flat shape with three straight sides and three corners ▲
2 a metal musical instrument of this shape, played by striking it with a metal rod

trick

1 to cheat
2 something clever done either to cheat or to amuse people

trickle

a very small flow of a liquid

trifle

1 a small thing of no importance
2 a kind of dessert made of cake, custard, fruit and cream

trip

1 a journey, especially one for pleasure
2 to fall

trolley

a small light cart pushed by hand (at the supermarket, for example)

trot

to move gently with short steps (quicker than walking, slower than running)

trouble

1 a worry; a problem; a difficulty
2 to worry or to annoy someone

trousers

a piece of clothing for the legs and the lower part of the body

trout

a kind of fish that lives in fresh water

truck

a vehicle that carries heavy things

true

correct; honest

trumpet

a metal musical instrument that you play by blowing

trunk

1 the thick stem of a tree
2 a large box for carrying things
3 an elephant's long nose

trunks

shorts worn by men and boys for swimming

trust

to believe that someone is honest

truth

what is true

try

to make an effort to do something

a
b
c
d
e
f
g
h
i
j
k
l
m
n
o
p
q
r
s
t T
u
v
w
x
y
z

T-shirt

a light cotton shirt with short sleeves and no collar

tub

a round container with an open top

tube

1 a thin hollow pipe
2 a soft plastic container from which the contents can be squeezed (for example, toothpaste)
3 the railway in London that goes under the ground

tug

to pull hard and sharply

tulip tulips

a kind of spring flower grown from a bulb

tumble

to fall heavily

tummy

see stomach

tune

a set of musical notes that sound pleasant together

tunnel

a covered road or path under the ground (through hills, for example)

turban

a long piece of cloth that some Asian men wrap around their heads

turkey

a large bird kept on farms

turn

1 to face a different way; to move around
2 to change direction
3 a chance to do something after other people have had a go

turnip

a root vegetable that is white or yellowish inside

turtle

an animal with a hard rounded shell that lives mainly in the sea

a
b
c
d
e
f
g
h
i
j
k
l
m
n
o
p
q
r
s
t T
u
v
w
x
y
z

tusk

a long slightly curved and pointed tooth found in an animal such as an elephant

twice

two times

twig

a very small branch of a tree

twinkle

to shine with small bright flashes

twins

two people born at the same time to the same mother

twist

1   to turn something (a bottle cap, for example)
2   a turn

type

1   a special sort; a kind
2   to tap keys on a computer keyboard so as to make words

tyre

the rubber round the outside of a wheel, often filled with air

ugly

not nice to look at

umbrella

a long stick with a covering that you hold over your head to keep off the rain

uncle

the brother of a father or mother; an aunt's husband

under

1   covered by
2   below; less than

underpants (pants)

what you wear underneath your trousers or skirt

understand

to know what something means

unfair

not fair

a
b
c
d
e
f
g
h
i
j
k
l
m
n
o
p
q
r
s
t
u U
v
w
x
y
z

a
b
c
d
e
f
g
h
i
j
k
l
m
n
o
p
q
r
s
t
u U
v
w
x
y
z

unhappy

not happy

unicorn

an imaginary animal that looks like a horse with one long horn

uniform

special clothes worn by children who go to the same school or club, or by people who work together (nurses, for example)

unpleasant

nasty; not pleasant

until

up to the time of

unwell

ill

up

to a higher place

upon

on; on top of

upright

straight up

upset

1 to make others unhappy
2 to knock over

upside down

the wrong way up

upstairs

on a higher floor of a building

urgent

so important that it needs to be done at once

use (say 'yooz')

to do something with

use (say 'yoos')

what you do with something

useful

of some use; helpful

useless

of no use; not useful

usual

often done; happening often

vV

valley
low ground between two hills or mountains

valuable
1 very useful
2 worth a lot of money

van

a vehicle for carrying things

vanish
to go out of sight; to disappear

vase
a container for holding flowers

vegetable vegetables (veg)

a plant grown for food (for example, a carrot or a cabbage)

vegetarian
a person who does not eat meat or fish

vehicle
a machine used for carrying people or things (for example, a car or a van)

velvet
a kind of cloth that is soft and smooth on one side

verse
1 a poem
2 one part of a poem

vest

a piece of clothing worn next to the skin on the top part of the body, to keep you warm

vet
a doctor for animals

vicar
a priest in the Church of England

victory
when a person or a group of people beats others in battle or in a competition

a b c d e f g h i j k l m n o p q r s t u v V w x y z

a b c d e f g h i j k l m n o p q r s t u **v V** w x y z

video

a film for showing on a television

video camera

a camera that films movements and records sounds

view

1 what you can see
2 what you think about something

village

a number of houses grouped together; a small town

vinegar

a sour liquid used for flavouring and for preserving food

violence

1 strong force
2 wild and hurtful behaviour

violet

1 a tiny purple flower
2 a purple colour, one of the colours of the rainbow

violin

a musical instrument with four strings, held under the chin and played with a bow

visit

to go and see someone or something

voice

the sound you make when you speak or sing

volcano

a mountain that sometimes throws out melting rock, hot ash, steam and flames

volume

1 the space something fills
2 a book
3 how loud a sound is

voyage

a long journey, usually by sea

vulture

a large bird that feeds on dead animals

wW

wade
to walk through water or mud

wafer

a very thin biscuit sometimes eaten with ice cream

wage
money given for work done

waist
the middle of the body

wait
to stay in a place for a reason

waiter

a man who serves food and drinks in a restaurant or café

waitress
a woman who serves food and drinks in a restaurant or café

wake
to stop sleeping

walk

to move on the feet

wall
the bricks that make the side of a building, a room or a piece of land

wallet

a small flat case for money or cards, usually carried in the pocket

wallpaper
paper that covers the walls of a room

a b c d e f g h i j k l m n o p q r s t u v w W x y z

a
b
c
d
e
f
g
h
i
j
k
l
m
n
o
p
q
r
s
t
u
v
w W
x
y
z

walnut

a kind of nut

wand

a thin straight stick used by magicians and fairies

wander

to move about slowly

want

to wish to have

war

fighting between countries or large groups of people

ward

a room with beds at a hospital

wardrobe

a cupboard for storing clothes

warm

fairly hot

warn

to tell someone about a possible difficulty or danger

wash

to clean using water

wasp

an insect with black and yellow stripes and a painful sting

waste

1 rubbish
2 to use more things than you really need

watch

1 a small clock, usually worn on the wrist
2 to look at carefully
3 to guard

water

the liquid that is found in rivers and in the sea, and falls as rain

wave

1 to put one arm up and move your hand quickly from side to side to be friendly
2 a moving line of water (on the sea or on a lake, for example)
3 the way that energy sometimes travels

wax

a fatty material used to make candles and polish

way

1 how you do something
2 a road or path

weak

not strong

weapon

a tool you use to fight or hunt with

wear

1 to have something on (for example, clothes or jewellery)
2 slight damage caused by a lot of use

weasel

a small and furry wild animal with a long body

weather

how sunny, cold or wet it is outside

weave

to make cloth by twisting threads over and under each other

web

1 short for **cobweb**
2 another name for the **internet**

website

a place on the internet where you can find information

wedding

when two people get married

weed

1 a wild plant that grows where it is not wanted
2 to dig out weeds

week

seven days

weekend

the two days at the end of a week: Saturday and Sunday

weep

to cry

weigh

1 to measure how heavy something is
2 to be a certain weight

a b c d e f g h i j k l m n o p q r s t u v w **W** x y z

a
b
c
d
e
f
g
h
i
j
k
l
m
n
o
p
q
r
s
t
u
v
w W
x
y
z

weight

how heavy something is

welcome

to be friendly and show you are
happy when someone comes

well

1   a deep hole holding water
2   in good health
3   in a good way

wellingtons (wellies)

long rubber boots

west

the direction where the
sun goes down

wet

having a lot of liquid in it
or on it

whale

the largest sea animal

wheat

a plant producing grain that
is used to make flour

wheel

1   a circle of metal, plastic or
    wood that turns and
    helps you to move things
    more easily
2   to push something
    that has wheels

wheelbarrow

a small cart that you use to
carry things (in the garden,
for example)

wheelchair

a chair with wheels that is used
by people who cannot walk

wheelie bin

a large bin on wheels

whimper

to cry softly

whip

to stir something round
and round when you
are preparing food

whirl (say 'wurl')

to spin round quickly

whiskers

long stiff hairs on the face
(of a cat, for example)

whisper

to speak very quietly

whistle

1 a high shrill note made by
   blowing through the lips
   or teeth
2 an instrument that you
   blow to make a high note

white

1 the colour of clean snow
2 the part of an egg
   round the yolk

whole

complete; with nothing missing

wicked

very bad; evil

wide

not narrow

wife

a married woman

wig

false hair to cover the head

wild

1 not tame; fierce
2 not looked after by people
3 out of control

win

to be first in a competition
or race

wind (sounds like 'p**inned**')

air that is moving quickly

wind (sounds like 'm**ind**')

to turn round and round

a
b
c
d
e
f
g
h
i
j
k
l
m
n
o
p
q
r
s
t
u
v
w **W**
x
y
z

windmill

a building with sails that turn round and round in the wind

window

a gap in the wall of a building that lets light in

wine

a strong drink made from the juice of crushed fruit

wing

1 the part of a bird or insect that is used for flying
2 the part of a plane that keeps it in the air

wink

to shut and open one eye

winner

the person who wins a competition or race

winter

the coldest season of the year, between autumn and spring

wipe

to dry or clean with a cloth

wire

thin metal thread

wise

clever; understanding a lot

wish

1 to want very much, especially something you are unlikely to get
2 what you wish for

witch

in stories, a woman who can use magic to do things

wizard

in stories, a man who can use magic to do things

wolf

a wild animal like a large dog

woman

an adult female person

wonder (say 'wunder')

1 to be surprised at
2 to want to know

wonderful

very good or pleasant; amazing

wood

1 a lot of trees growing together
2 the material that trees are made of

wool

1 thread used in weaving or knitting
2 the thick hair on the backs of sheep and lambs

word

letters put together so that they mean something

work

something you do; your job

world

the earth

worm

a long thin animal with a soft body that lives in soil

worn

when something has been used so much that it is of little more use

worry

to be afraid that something may go wrong

worse

not as good as; less well

worship

to show that you believe someone to be very good and very important

worth

value

wound (say 'woond')

a place where the skin of a person or animal has been cut

wrap

to put a covering closely round something

a
b
c
d
e
f
g
h
i
j
k
l
m
n
o
p
q
r
s
t
u
v
w **W**
x
y
z

a
b
c
d
e
f
g
h
i
j
k
l
m
n
o
p
q
r
s
t
u
v
w
x X
y
z

wreck

1 to smash completely
2 something that has been smashed (for example, a car or a ship that cannot be used any more)

wren

a kind of very small brown bird

wrestle

to struggle with a person and try to throw him or her to the ground

wriggle

to twist the body about

wrist

the joint between the hand and the arm

write

to put words or letters on paper so that they can be read

wrong

not right; not correct

X-ray

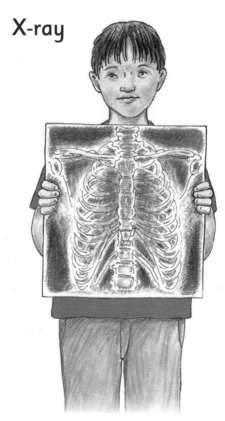

a special photograph of the inside of your body

xylophone (say 'zylophone')

a musical instrument played by hitting bars of wood or metal with a small hammer

yY

yacht (say 'yot')
a light sailing boat, often used for racing

yard
1 a measure of length that is a bit less than one metre
2 a piece of ground next to a building with a fence or wall around it

yarmulke

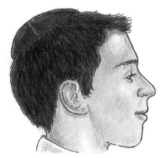

a small cap worn on the head by some Jewish men

yawn
to open the mouth and breathe in and out deeply, usually when tired or bored

year
a length of time equal to 12 months; the time that the earth takes to go once round the sun

yell
to shout very loudly

yellow
the colour of a lemon or the yolk of an egg

yesterday
the day before today

yogurt

a sour food made from milk, often sweetened with sugar and sometimes flavoured with fruit

yolk
the yellow centre part of an egg

young
not old

youth
1 the time when you are young
2 a young man

yo-yo

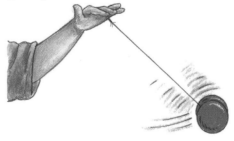

a toy that moves up and down a string

a b c d e f g h i j k l m n o p q r s t u v w x y z Z

zZ

zebra

an African animal like a small horse with black and white stripes

zebra crossing

a part of the street specially marked with stripes, for people to cross

zigzag

to move sharply to one side and then to the other

zimmer

a kind of walking frame often used by people who find walking difficult

zinc

a whitish metal

zip

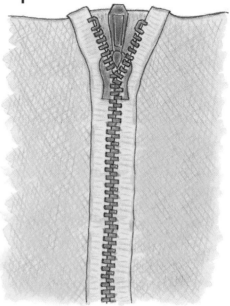

a sliding device used to do up some of your clothes

zone

an area; a part of a town or a country

zoo

a place where wild animals are kept so that people can look at them

Months of the year

January

February

March

April

May

June

July

August

September

October

November

December

Days of the week

Monday

Tuesday

Wednesday

Thursday

Friday

Saturday

Sunday

Colours

black

blue

brown

green

grey

lilac

orange

pink

purple

red

yellow

white

Numbers

1 one

2 two

3 three

4 four

5 five

6 six

7 seven

8 eight

9 nine

10 ten

11 eleven

12 twelve

13 thirteen

14 fourteen

15 fifteen

16 sixteen

17 seventeen

18 eighteen

19 nineteen

20 twenty

21 twenty-one

30 thirty

40 forty

50 fifty

60 sixty

70 seventy

80 eighty

90 ninety

100 one hundred

101 one hundred and one

200 two hundred

1000 one thousand

10 000 ten thousand

100 000 one hundred thousand

1 000 000 one million